PARENTING
at Your BEST

PARENTING at Your BEST

Powerful Reflections and Straightforward Tips
for Becoming a Mindful Parent

RONI WING LAMBRECHT
In Loving Memory of Dalton John Lambrecht

Parenting at Your Best:
Powerful Reflections and Straightforward Tips for Becoming a Mindful Parent
Published by 3 Hearts Press
Castle Rock, CO

Copyright ©2017 Roni Wing Lambrecht. All rights reserved.

No part of this book may be reproduced or transmitted in any form or by any means, mechanical or electronic, including photocopying or recording, or by any information storage or retrieval system, or transmitted by email without permission in writing from the publisher/author, except by a reviewer who may quote passages in a review.

All images, logos, quotes, and trademarks included in this book are subject to use according to trademark and copyright laws of the United States of America.

Library of Congress Control Number: 2016912982

ISBN: 978-0-9979298-0-5

Wing Lambrecht, Roni, Author
Parenting at Your Best:
Powerful Reflections and Straightforward Tips for Becoming a Mindful Parent
Roni Wing Lambrecht
FAMILY & RELATIONSHIPS / Parenting

Cover Design: Roni Lambrecht and Victoria Wolf of Red Wolf Publishing
Cover Photos: Glamis Sand Dunes by Roni Lambrecht / Photo of Lambrecht Family by Andy & Angie Wood of A&A Photography
Book Design & Layout: Roni Wing Lambrecht and Andrea Costantine
Author's Photo: Britt Nemeth Photography
Editors: Pamela Kirby, Donna Mazzitelli, Vicki Tosher
Publishing Consultant: Polly Letofsky of My Word Publishing

QUANTITY PURCHASES:
Schools, companies, professional groups, clubs, and other organizations may qualify for special terms when ordering quantities of this title. For information, email DoItForDalton@gmail.com.

DISCLAIMER:
Neither the author nor the publisher assumes any responsibility for errors, omissions, or contrary interpretations of the subject matter herein.
Any perceived slight of any individual or organization is purely unintentional.

All rights reserved by Roni Wing Lambrecht and 3 Hearts Press
This book is printed in the United States of America.

This book is for those who have stood by us
in the life we never imagined we would be living without Dalton.
Thank you for your love, support, and guidance.
Without you all, our continuing existence would not be possible.

To Dalton's Friends...
Thank you for your love, friendship, and support of Dalton
during the short years that you knew him,
and for all the support you've shown to us since he has been gone.
One of Dalton's biggest fears was knowing that his tight-knit
group of friends might lose connection after graduation.
Please make sure you all keep in touch
and support each other in your new endeavors,
knowing he's right there with you.
Live your life to the fullest, keeping your family and friends close,
sharing your heart with those around you,
giving life all you've got to give.
Live it without regrets.
If you need help, ask for it.
If you're happy, share it with those around you.
If you love someone, tell them!
Most important, if Dalton, or anyone else,
has ever helped you on your journey,
thank them and take that experience
and Pay It Forward to someone else who needs
a smile, a hug, a good listener, or a good friend.
We would do anything to have Dalton moving forward in this life with
all of you, so we're hoping you will do your best to carry on his legacy
and celebrate him by doing something special
for someone else today and every day.

With Love, Roni & John Lambrecht,
in loving memory of our Dalton.

Dalton and John - 2/7/2000 (upper left), Dalton and Roni - 2/7/2000 (upper right), JRD in Glamis 12/25/2013 (bottom)

For our Sugarbear, Sug, Angel, Punk, Punkin, Cuddlebug, Jeepers, DJ, Deej, Deejer, Dalton John Lambrecht:

You'll always be my baby, even when you're old ...

Thank you for all the life lessons.
I know I wasn't always the best mommy,
but I sure hope you know I tried my very best.
You are the biggest and best accomplishment
of our lives,
and the best love story we'll ever know.
Dad and I are counting every second of every day
until we get to be with you again.
Please always remember,
I love you more than you love me,
cuz I love you to infinity ...
and beyond!

Love,
Mom, Mommy, Mum, Ma, Madre
&
Dad, Daddy, Da-Dee, Pappi

Contents

Preface   13
Introduction   19

1   Write Your Way Into My Heart   33
2   Time of My Life   45
3   Squeeze My Stuffin's Out   49
4   Can I Be On Your Schedule?   53
5   Real Life Business Card   61
6   Speak Up!   65
7   Do You Hear What I Hear?   71
8   I've Got a Feeling   75
9   Something to Believe In   79
10 My Home Is Your Home Is Our Home   85
11 Get Real!   95
12 Follow Through   101
13 Use The Tools You Have Been Given   107
14 How Bad Do You Want It?   113
15 Respect - Bring It Back!   123

16	Daily Rituals and Traditions	127
17	Celebrate!	131
18	Time to Eat	137
19	Picture Perfect	145
20	Music to My Ears	149
21	Dance, Dance, Dance	155
22	Family Game Night	159
23	Words and Events That Alter Your Vocabulary	163
24	Road Trip!	169
25	Events That Transform Our Lives	173
26	Advance Arrangements	185
27	Pay It Forward	193
28	Feed The People Who Feed You	199
29	Common Sense Ain't So Common	205
30	Best Laid Plans	213

Epilogue	219
Acknowledgments	223
Discussion Guide	239
The Soundtrack of Our Lives with Dalton	246
Author Bio	249

Dalton - Age 2 - 8/31/2000 (top), Dalton in Glamis - 12/25/2013 (middle),
JRD in Moab - 5/2009 (bottom)

Preface

We were blessed to have a beautiful son, Dalton, in 1998. Since then, we've spent most of our free time camping and riding 4-wheelers; so much so, that we had Dalton riding at 7 weeks old (yes, 7 weeks). He got his own 4-wheeler on his 10th birthday and by age 15, he was an expert rider.

In December 2013, we took a vacation to Glamis, California, to camp and ride at the Imperial Sand Dunes. It was the first Christmas just the three of us had ever spent together, and it was awesome!

On Sunday, December 29th, five days into our vacation, Dalton was enjoying a ride practicing jumps and wheelies when he was hit head-on by a sandrail. His death was instant, and Dalton went to Heaven enjoying what he loved. For that, we are grateful.

As we look back on Dalton's life and our time with him, thoughts and emotions often take over logic, and we begin thinking of the things he will miss here - getting his drivers' license, graduating with his friends, heading off to the Marines, etc. At those times, in particular, we have to step back and realize how blessed we were to have him as our *only* child and how blessed he was to have us for his parents. We had a full life in our little family of three, and we made a great team together.

We often hear from family and friends that they never knew a more close-knit family than ours. We love to hear that, because when we look back on all that was and could have been, regrets and sadness could overtake us. Yet we have so much to be thankful for …

*15 years, 8 months, 3 days, 15 hours, and 37 minutes
with the best son anyone could ever dream of having …*

That said, we often speak with people who tell us they have regrets about their life – the way they are living it, how they wish they had chosen a different career path, how they wish they had planned better for retirement, etc. Mostly, though, we hear people say they have regrets about parenting. It could be we hear that more now because of our current situation, but we do feel like it's an important topic to discuss as parents and also as a community.

As first-time parents, we often believe that we have parenthood planned out perfectly, yet it seems that *nothing* in parenting goes as planned, thus causing us to react in moments of chaos prompting regrets later (sometimes within the second we said or did something, without having taken the time to think it through). I found this during pregnancy, in the delivery room, and every step of the way after Dalton's entrance into this big, crazy, chaotic world. My husband, John, struggles with his regrets on a daily basis. In fact, in a round-about way, this book was his idea, as he wants to do whatever it takes to help other parents spend quality time with their kids so they can avoid living with the same regrets he has. I am thankful John has allowed me to be his voice in this process.

One of the things we hope to do on our grief journey is to help parents and kids be *better* parents and *better* kids; to live their lives together *without regrets,* or at least *very few* regrets.

In each chapter, I'll share photos and quotes that were often printed, laminated, and hung on our fridge, as well as songs that we used to sing together, and those that make us think of Dalton now. More important, I'll share some of the things we *think* we did *well* in our job as first-time parents and also some experiences we *learned from.*

Our wish is to give you some of the tools we had (or wish we'd had) to be an amazing influence in your children's lives. While it would be overwhelming to consider the implementation of *every* idea shared in this book, please flag the ideas that seem meaningful to you as you read. Once you have finished the book, select two or three of those ideas to implement now. Then, set yourself a reminder to consider implementing a couple more of the identified items six months from now, and every six months after that. There's also a worksheet on my website at www.ParentingAtYourBestWithoutRegrets.com which is intended to help guide you into implementing the most meaningful ideas a few at a time. You can even download it now and keep it with you as you read the book. Additionally, there is a Discussion Guide at the end of the book and continually updated discussion topics are available on the website, in case you would like to use them in a group setting, like a parenting group or a book club.

PREFACE

With love and best wishes for a long, happy life with your babies, and their babies, and beyond,

Dalton's Parents,
Roni & John Lambrecht

> Song: When I See You Smile
> Written by Diane Warren
> Performed by Bad English

JRD - Blake Shelton Cruise - Miami, FL - 10/21/2012

Introduction

Think Before You Start Making Babies: The Parenting Plan

For many, becoming a parent happens easily, and for others, it takes a lot of time, effort, and expense. Either way, becoming a parent is the most important opportunity anyone could ever have the honor of experiencing in their lifetime. It should be approached with *extreme* care and concern. There are so many things to think about; things we don't often realize will be important until it's too late. Being pro-active is the best way to approach *everything* having to do with making babies.

Something I wish we had done sooner, rather than later, was to create a parenting plan to include several topics. We waited until Dalton was in elementary school to come up with our first outline. I am touching briefly on the topics listed below, but you'll want to spend some quality time reviewing them for your own plan and adjust it regularly based on your family's needs. I would put this on your calendar as something to be discussed at least twice per year after the baby is born.

What Do You Want for Your Child?

It's important you know *why* you want to become a parent and what your goals are for your child. Is it the dream of the big house with the white picket fence, or is it that you want a mini-me running around? Are you having a child because that's what's expected or was this a surprise? Do you want your child to have more opportunities than you did while you were growing up? If so, how will you lead them to those opportunities? Is it important they graduate from high school and attend college, or would you rather they join the military? What importance will you place on the simple idea of your child just growing up to be happy and self-sufficient?

> Becoming a parent is the most important opportunity anyone could ever have the honor of experiencing in their lifetime.

Granted, we cannot make our children do exactly what we want them to do, but we can certainly plan accordingly and hope for the best. Parenting will throw many unanticipated curves your way, and it's important to know your intentions *before* you enter into the world of parenting. Why? Because when times get tough, you must remind yourself of your original objective. It's a fact that there will be days you just want to give up, yet walking away is *not an option*; adjusting your plan *is*.

Love

There's an anonymous quote that says, "The greatest gift a father can give his children is to love their mother." (And vice-versa!) This is so true! As parents, we want to give our kids *everything* we can afford, yet the one thing they really need isn't something we can buy for them at all. It's the love of each other and family.

Children need to be shown that true love *is* possible, that it takes effort and dedication and clear communication, and, even when times are tough, it's always important to show them that love prevails. I have seen people still madly in love after 65 years of marriage, and I've seen others where their marriages have failed, yet each parent still shows the other respect and love in their dealings with one another in front of the children.

It's important to realize that what we present to our children in our relationships is what they will often look for in their own relationships as they grow. *Show* them what you want them to learn about relationships by being the person you want them to fall in love with in the future.

Finances

Finances play a huge role in the decision to have a child. It's been said that if you wait until you're financially stable, you'll never have children. That could be true, but it *is* of the highest importance to make sure you and your partner can truly afford a baby, financially and emotionally, *before* you make one. If you're adult enough to create the expense, you must be able to pay for it yourself, without help from your family or other taxpayers.

Birth or Adoption

Giving birth to your own child is usually the preferred method, yet I've heard many people discuss the amazing gift of adoption as well. Both should be researched and decided upon together.

INTRODUCTION

Birthing Preferences

There are lots of choices. There are medical issues such as which OBGYN to use (get references!), the hospital you'd like to be in, and whether or not to have an epidural. There are more personal things too: will you allow your partner to video the birth? Who will you want to attend? Who will be invited afterward? Actively partake in discussions with your partner ahead of time and put them in writing. Discuss them *again and again,* as your choices may change as the birth date gets closer.

Names

Will the baby/babies be given family names or will you find them from a baby name book? Will you look online for the most popular/least popular names? Make sure you choose at least one name (preferably two) for each sex. Write the names down and put them in your hospital bag as you may be surprised. We've had many folks tell us that the name they originally chose did not at all resemble their baby once it was born, so they changed it. Yet, others who anticipated a girl and were surprised by a boy, and vice-versa. It's always good to be over-prepared.

Religion & Politics

Both are very touchy topics and need to be addressed clearly by both parents, and, often their families as well. Enough said.

Discipline

Discuss how you believe children should be disciplined. How were you raised? How was your partner raised? Do you believe in spanking, sitting a child in the corner, reasoning with them, or just telling them how it is? Every child is different, and circumstances change actions. It's important that you discuss this in detail with your partner on a regular basis, or it will inevitably create conflicts in front of your children. One thing that is very important to remember is to make sure that when your child misbehaves, both you and your child understand that, while their behavior was bad, they, themselves, are not a bad person.

Family Dynamics

Let's be honest. Every family has a little bit of crazy (sometimes *a lot* of it!). Plan *together* now how you will approach tough situations with difficult family members.

Will you stand up for your partner/back them up? Will you allow parents/siblings to interfere with your actions and beliefs? Be strong and confident in your joint beliefs and be fully supportive of each other. This family, *the one with the baby*, should *always* take priority. No exceptions.

Immunizations, Circumcision, and Breastfeeding

I mentioned family dynamics just before this paragraph because it's often the family that causes strife when it comes to discussing immunizations, circumcisions, and breastfeeding. As for breastfeeding, make choices based on what you know *now*, as the way your baby reacts to breastfeeding will make this decision for you in the long run. Don't force it. I've had friends who breastfed their kids for years and others who couldn't produce enough milk to make it happen the first day. In my case, Dalton refused to "latch-on," so we were forced to go another direction. Be patient. You *do* have choices, and the choices you make won't be right or wrong. They will just be the choices you make and feel most comfortable with. Do the research and trust your instincts (there's a lot of that in parenting).

Language

Does everyone in your household speak the same language, or are there multiple languages spoken in your home? If there are multiple, then you need to discuss which languages will be spoken to and around the child, and how it will affect *every* member of the household (including other siblings and family members who do not speak the other language).

When a foreign language is spoken around others who do not know that language, they often feel alienated, and you'll want to do all you can to be sure that does not happen, especially with other children.

Where Will You Live?

Does it make sense to stay where you are, live with your folks, move up to a larger home, move to another state where you might have more/less help from family and friends? These are all things that must be discussed before making a baby. As a REALTOR®, my experience tells me that you should do this before, or in the first three months of pregnancy. That way, the new mom has time to "nest" in the new location *before* the third trimester begins (having a mom who is 8 or 9 months pregnant looking for homes is not usually the happiest experience for mom, dad, or agent).

INTRODUCTION

Work/School

One of the most important discussions you will need to have is whether or not you will continue to have the same type of schedule you do now. Will you continue to work or go to school or whatever it is that you do *now*, even *after* the baby arrives?

Your money needs to come from somewhere and there needs to be enough of it to pay bills and put food on the table, but you also can't buy time, and spending quality time with your child and your partner is priceless. There *is* a happy medium. You just have to find it. Maybe one partner works during the day and the other at night and you have weekends together. Maybe you take six weeks off and go right back to work and the baby goes to daycare, and you see them at night and on weekends. There *are* ways to make it work. Discuss it and make a solid Plan A. Then have a Plan B and a Plan C, because *things will change* and you'll need to quickly define new ways of adapting.

Doctors & Daycare

Get references from highly trusted family and friends early in your pregnancy or adoption process. Use city, county, and state resources. Check online reviews. Visit and interview at least three of each. Trust your instincts.

Health Insurance

Make sure your insurance covers childbirth or adopted children immediately from the time of their birth/placement with you. As we all know, insurance coverage has changed a lot. Know your options inside and out.

Learning the Sex of the Baby

I am the ultimate planner. I plan *everything* to the nth degree, so much so that I drive the people around me crazy sometimes, especially my husband and my co-workers. So, when John and I announced we were pregnant, everyone who knew me was shocked to learn that I wanted to be surprised about the sex of the baby when the baby was born and *not a moment before.*

Maybe this was a test of faith or a test of myself to see if I could even handle the unknown (It was a huge test for this control freak!). Most of all, I thought it was an extremely special time in our marriage to trust in each other and have one last wonderful surprise in our lives that nobody else had control of. And, boy, was Dalton ever a surprise! When our OBGYN put Dalton on my chest and said, "It's a boy!" John and I were completely stunned. All the old wives' tales we had heard about the way the baby was sitting in my belly and the foods I'd been craving were all put to shame.

It was such an amazing experience to see each of our faces when we were asked what his name was going to be. We'd picked out a bunch of girl's names and never really decided on a boy's name at all. The one boy name we thought we both liked was "Dalton," so that's what we went with, and it was perfect.

That said, having the opportunity to dream and wonder about the gender of our soon-to-be bundle-of-joy gave John and I a great deal to talk about in the months before Dalton's arrival, which helped our relationship flourish even more. It also required us to be more creative in decorating the baby room and finding clothes and toys.

Many people plan every detail of their lives from schedules to food to clothes to friends. The opportunity to be happily surprised by not knowing the sex of your baby is *a gift that only your new baby can give you*. If I had it to do all over again, I'd do it exactly the same way. What will you choose to do?

Music

Play it loud. Play it often. Play every genre you enjoy. Put headphones on your tummy while you sleep (not too loud, though, as it echoes in the womb). You'll be amazed how much music becomes a part of the baby's life and all the memories you make together when they are in your tummy, and after. Enjoy it!

Estate Planning

Research and get references from highly trusted family and friends for a reputable attorney and financial planner. Meet with them both *at the same time with everyone in the same room* and get all the paperwork (wills, trusts, powers of attorney, etc.) done *before* the baby arrives. It's money well spent that can save you tons of time and heartache later. Ask for it as a baby gift. No excuses. Do it!

Divorce

While some marriages can end amicably, it's a fact that many end terribly, which has long and lasting consequences for all parties involved, especially the children. Make a pact with your partner in writing (maybe while writing your estate plan) stating that no matter what happens, you will never say rude things to, or about each other, in front of the children and that the children's needs and feelings will always come first. I'm not one for planning a downfall, but I've seen so much hatred between ex-spouses that I wonder if any of it could be changed if things were planned and in writing ahead of time while everyone was still friendly. Just a thought.

INTRODUCTION

Minor Stuff

Only after the above items are done do you focus on these...

Baby showers, registering for gifts, announcements, decorating the baby room, etc.

If all that didn't scare you away,
let's move on to the details...

> Song: Rich Man
> Written by Rory Lee & David Vincent
> Performed by Mark Wills

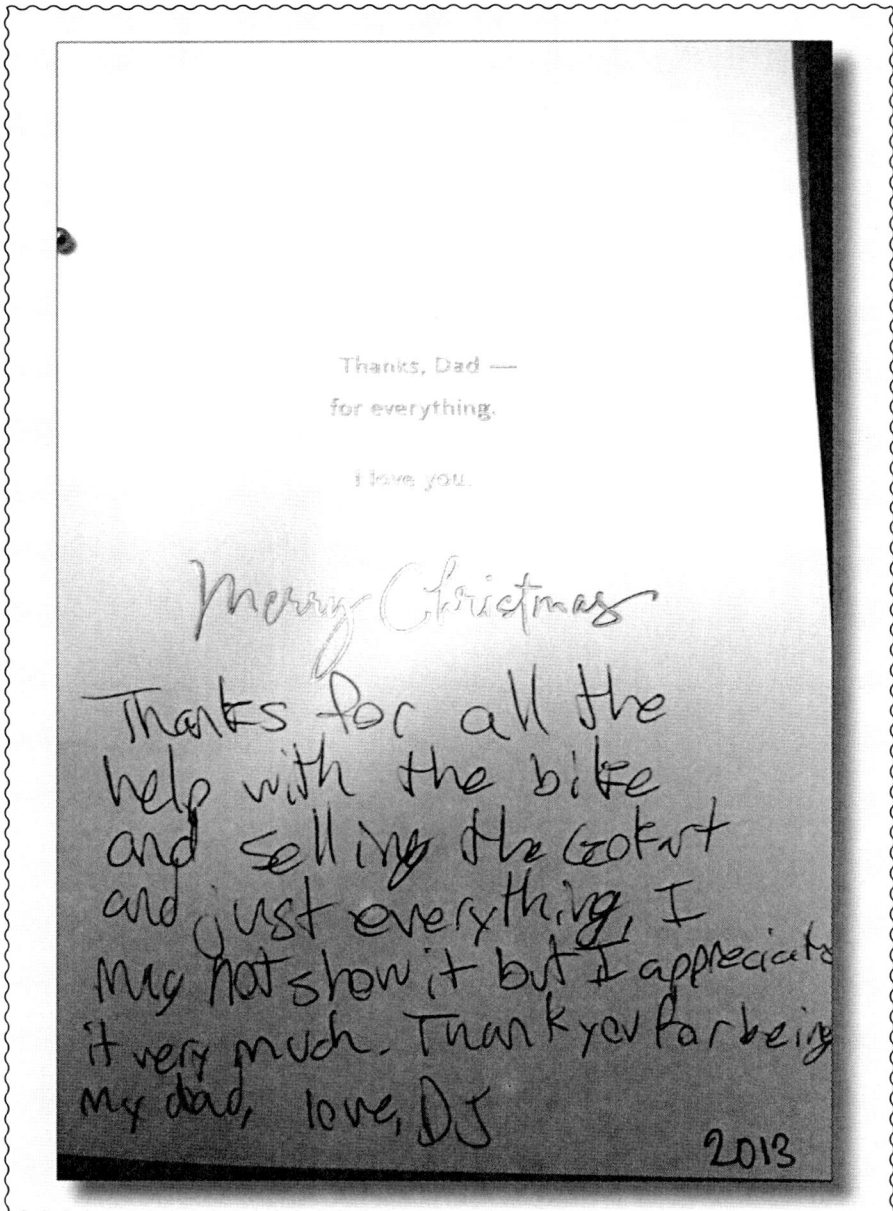

Dalton's last card to John...
"Thanks for all the help with the bike and selling the go-kart and just everything.
I may not not show it, but I appreciate it very much. Thank you for being my dad.
love, DJ"

Write Your Way Into My Heart

I am a firm believer that anyone can *say* anything, but it doesn't hold much worth until it's in writing, and so I begin with *Dalton's Journal;* one of the most important accomplishments of my life...

When I was pregnant, I began writing a journal to our baby. I started with how proud I was to be its mommy, how much I adored John, and how John was going to make such a great daddy. I told the baby about our lives, how we met and fell in love, what we hoped we could teach him/her, and how scared and excited we were to be parents.

While I didn't write in it as often as I should have, I wrote about a lot of things, like how tired I was, and what a struggle it was to raise a headstrong kid. I wrote about his laugh and his friends and school and teachers. More often than not, I would write funny stories about things Dalton said or things that had happened; things I would never want to forget (the stories that make you laugh out loud years later when you read them). As a parent, there are so many breathtaking memories that often get pushed aside because the daily minutia takes up so much of our brains. There are stories in that journal I wanted to remember forever when I wrote them down, and there are many that I had completely forgotten until I read them again after Dalton passed away.

> It has reminded us over and over what a full life we had with our angel and the strength of our love for one another.

When Dalton was about 8 or 9, he asked me what I was writing, and I told him I had been writing him a long love letter since before he was born. He wanted to read it *right then and there*. We even wrestled for it, but I won. I told him that he had to wait until his 18th birthday, and that, even then, it always had to "live" at my house so I could keep reading it too.

Since the accident, so much is a blur, yet there is no question in our minds that *Dalton's Journal* saved our marriage, and it has saved us so many times between then and now. It has reminded us over and over what a full life we had with our angel and the strength of our love for one another. This is how it happened...

My parents flew out to be with us after Dalton passed away and I hadn't been outside the camper, nor had I showered or eaten. My mom forced me into the shower and then dressed me. She made John do the same thing. Then she told us we had to go for a walk and get some fresh air. For some reason, I grabbed *Dalton's Journal* on the way out the door. After a while, we came to a beautiful sitting area where I sat down and opened it. I began reading and crying. John asked me if I would read it to him and I said, "No. This was for Dalton." John begged me, and so I began reading to him. The first several pages were written before Dalton was ever born. I had written all about John and I, how we fell in love, and how much we were looking forward to meeting our baby. I had also written how lucky the baby would be to have John as its daddy, how much I adored John, and how lucky I was to call him my husband and my best friend.

After I read several pages, John said, "I never knew you felt that way." I couldn't believe my ears! After all the years of cards and poems I had written him and the countless times I had told him directly how much I loved him, how did he not know this?!?! What?!?!

He said, "I never heard you tell anyone else that before." It was then and there, after nearly 20 years of marriage, that I felt like we completely understood each other. I believe Dalton had a hand in making me pick up his journal and read to John. The statistics of parents divorcing after they've lost their only child are staggering, and we're very blessed to still be together.

Straightforward Tips for Parenting at Your Best

I've always been a proponent of journaling and writing love letters to our kids (and requiring them to learn how to write back). Because of this, I have always given journals as baby gifts. In fact, my second and third books, *A Parents Guide for Journaling to Their Child* and *A Parent's Journal to Their Child* (available now!!!), are actually a guide and a parenting journal with advice and prompts to help parents everywhere write ongoing love letters to their kids.

So, please, if you don't do anything else, please do this...

Journal of Love Letters for Each Child

Get a journal for each of your kids and start writing in it. Take it from parents who know the value of great memories... Write your child love letters and share stories about funny things they say or do, how they look, and what they like to wear. Include funny reactions they have, daily routines, traditions, the music they love to listen to, songs you like to sing together, hobbies, habits, family, friends, teachers, neighbors, daily schedules, etc. Share stories about your love for your spouse/partner, how you met and fell in love. Share times you laugh and cry and struggle to keep your sanity because your child is driving you crazy. Share your personal goals and dreams, as well as those you wish for them. Be honest and forthcoming. Write about it all. This doesn't have to be a daily task, but it's important to write several times a year at the very least. So much happens that could easily be forgotten if it wasn't written down. I also made it a priority to write to Dalton anytime something really funny or "big" happened.

Other great writing endeavors; all of which will take some guidance from you to your kids...

Thankful Journal

Start a Thankful Journal that you each write in every night before bed. All three of us had matching notebooks, and the process was as follows. Every night before bed, we sat on Dalton's bed and wrote in our Thankful Journals:

- ♥ Today, I am thankful for...
- ♥ Five good things about today were...
- ♥ Something I like about myself is...

For us, this only lasted a few months, but it was a good training tool to get us to talk about things more often and with more clarity. I wish I could say this was my idea, but if I remember correctly, this idea came from an Oprah show.

Story Journal

We have a good friend that told us about this one that she does with her grandkids.

- ♥ Writer 1: Writes the beginning of a story (1-2 pages), then gives the journal to Writer 2.
- ♥ Writer 2: Reads Writer 1's story and writes the

ending (1-2 pages), then turns the page and starts a completely new story (1-2 pages), then gives the journal to Writer 1.
- ♥ Writer 1: Reads the entire story that they wrote together and gives it a title, then reads Writer 2's new story and writes the ending (1-2 pages), then turns the page and starts a completely new story (1-2 pages), then gives the journal to Writer 2.
- ♥ Writer 2: Reads the entire story that they wrote together and gives it a title, then reads Writer 1's new story and writes the ending (1-2 pages), then turns the page and starts a completely new story (1-2 pages), then gives the journal to Writer 1.

You can come up with your own idea of how to do it, but the idea is that the stories go back and forth and, as the kids grow, you will clearly see how their writing and imagination improves.

Appreciation Journal

I've seen this done with parents and kids, grandparents and grandchildren, between bosses and co-workers, and between teachers and students. The idea is to write something nice about someone and give it to them. It could be as simple as telling your child you think they did a great job in an activity or thanking them for helping out without being asked. Then you give it to them, and later they'll return it to you thanking you just for being you or doing something nice for them. These are great for kids who have a hard time expressing their feelings face to face, and they help everyone appreciate the good in life, versus dwelling on the bad.

Vacation Journals

Before each family vacation or camping trip, get a small notebook and have your children write in it each day or night of the trip to explain what they did, who they were with, what they enjoyed and what they didn't, food they ate, etc. They can also draw pictures of the daily events. Not only will you be able to see how their writing/drawing progresses over the years, but you will also be helping them learn how to express themselves and improve their writing. It can also be very helpful years later if you ever have questions about where or when a photo was taken, what you did while you were there, or who was on the trip with you.

Birthday Envelopes

This is a great idea I found on social media...

Every year, on their birthday, write a letter to your child (grandchild, niece, nephew, neighbor, etc.) and add a small amount of cash to the envelope with the letter. Do this each year and give all the envelopes to your child for graduation. They'll get 17 or 18 years of letters, a good amount of cash, and they'll have a graduation present that lasts a lifetime.

Birthday, Greeting, and Thank You Cards

I have always been a stickler about writing nice cards. Dalton learned from an early age that before special days for others, he was expected to write a nice card to them. He also knew that after every birthday and Christmas, he'd be spending at least an hour writing personalized thank-you cards for the gifts he received and places he got to go. He loathed it at first, but then found it to be fun and started writing poetry and goofy stories in his cards to tell people what he used his gift for. My parents actually have all of the cards Dalton gave them hanging on their wall, including the one where he wrote, *"It's a pleasure being your grandson."* (That was one we all thought was pretty cute!) Additionally, I always explained to Dalton the importance of appreciating and validating someone and making sure to write something special in each card he wrote so that his words *mattered* and they were *worth reading.* Not to mention, I thought it was important that I raise a young man who knows how to write a love letter to his own wife and children in the future.

When Dalton was 14, he wrote me this amazing birth-

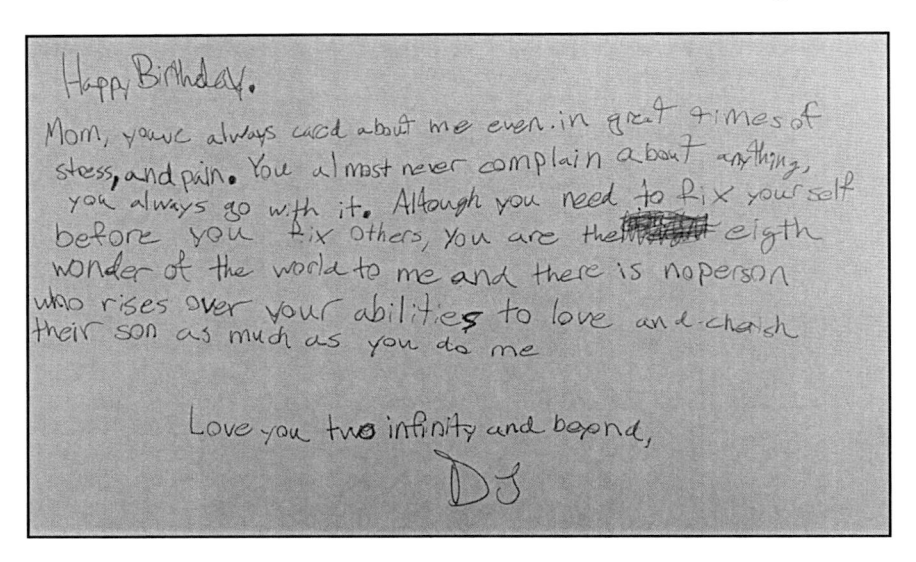

> Happy Birthday.
>
> Mom, you've always cared about me even in great times of stress, and pain. You almost never complain about anything, you always go with it. Although you need to fix yourself before you fix others, you are the eigth wonder of the world to me and there is no person who rises over your abilities to love and cherish their son as much as you do me.
>
> Love you two infinity and beyond,
>
> DJ

day card...

Since receiving this card, it has been my most prized possession. I am so blessed to have had a child who used his talents and teachings to write down his love for me so plainly. Someday soon, it will be tattooed on my right arm.

To teach your children, grandchildren, nieces, nephews, and friends this valuable lesson, try this...

1. Make sure you lead by example by writing them nice cards.
2. Along with their gifts for each birthday and holiday, give each child a box of thank you cards and stamps so they have them handy after the holiday. They might just surprise you!

> Song: *You'll Be In My Heart*
> Written and Performed by Phil Collins

Dalton & Roni - Blake Shelton Cruise - 10/19/2012

Time of My Life

Ever since Dalton was a toddler sleeping in his own bed, we always had "cuddle time." Every night, before John and I went to bed, we met in Dalton's bed with me on one side, Dalton in the middle, and John on the other side "sandwiching" Dalton. After he became a teenager, the title changed to, "hanging out," but it was all the same; it just had an enhanced title.

We'd have tickle wars, squishing wars, rolling wars, and pillow fights, sing songs, and talk about our lives, school, work, friends, teachers, bosses, etc. Then, when it was time to settle down, we would all get as close as we could possibly get and just cuddle. The feel of their hands, their breathing, how they sound when they're asleep - it's the most content feeling in the universe.

All in all, when I look back on our life with Dalton, these are the times that mean the most to me. No electronics or interruptions. Just one-on-one completely focused time with each other. It was the safest, most wonderful place I have ever been and I would give *anything* to go back to those nights. Life is just too long without them.

Straightforward Tips for Parenting at Your Best

> The feel of their hands, their breathing, how they sound when they're asleep - it's the most content feeling in the universe.

During "cuddle time," we always discussed our highs and lows of the day. We weren't just asking Dalton his highs and lows; we *all* shared our highs and lows. This helped Dalton to know that we weren't attacking him with questions about his day (this is especially important during the teen years). It also reminded him that we're people too, and we have lives outside of what he sees at home. And, while it may seem silly, sometimes telling a problem to your child makes it not seem like such a big problem anymore. In some cases, they even have great ideas about how to simply manage a problem that, as adults, we missed because we were too caught up in the details.

Take a *minimum* of ten minutes *every single night* and do this with each one of your kids. You can thank me later.

> Song: You're Gonna Miss This
> Written by Ashley Gorley
> & Lee Thomas Miller
> Performed by Trace Adkins

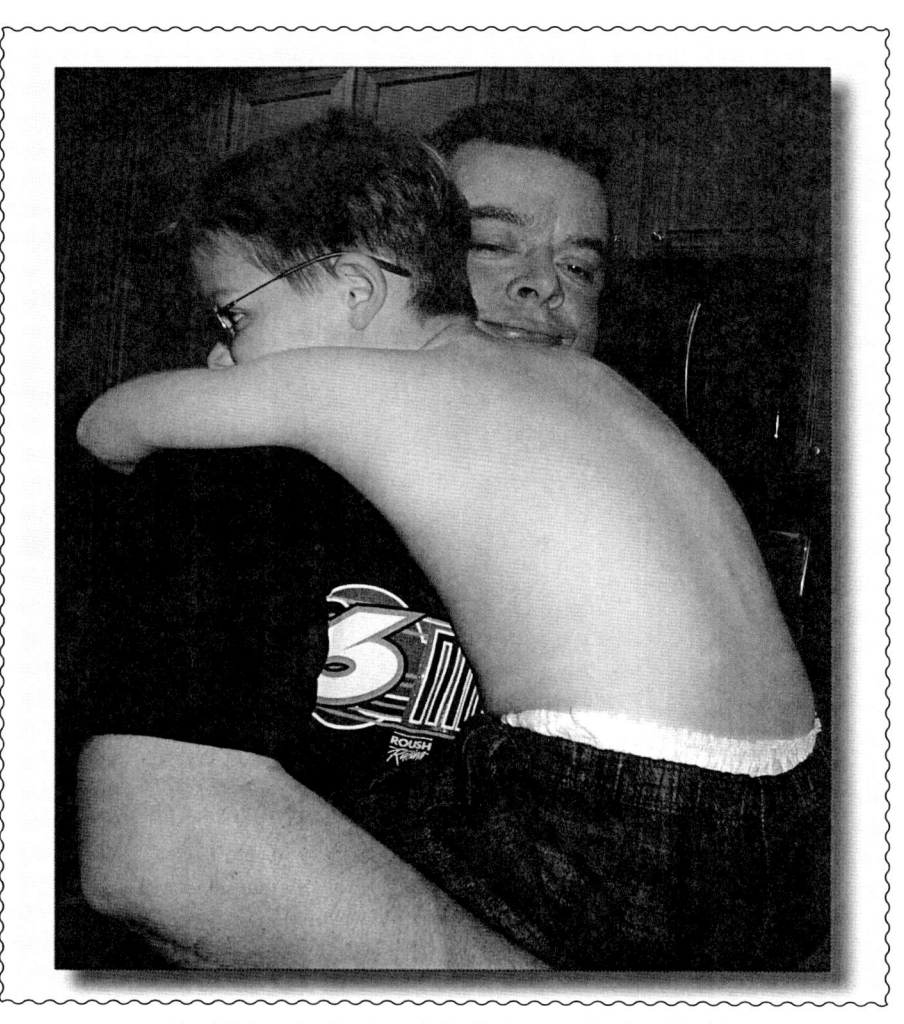

John & Dalton dancing through the kitchen on Dalton's 7th birthday

Squeeze My Stuffin's Out

Hugging properly is a true gift, yet it *can* be taught to willing participants. I lucked out having a child who loved to cuddle and hug. Dalton had friends who were not as talented in that department, so he taught them. One of the things nearly everyone discussed at his life celebration was how "he gave the best hugs!" and how his hugs always made you feel like you were the *only* person in his life.

Straightforward Tips for Parenting at Your Best

When you're hugging someone, wrap your arms completely around them, fold your head and neck into them, and squeeeeeeeze their stuffin's out. Hugging is no time to be a robot! And, if someone is doing it wrong, teach them how to hug properly. The world needs more great huggers!

> Song: Close To You
> Written by Burt Bacharach and Hal David
> Performed by The Carpenters

John and Dalton in the trackhoe - 2/7/2000 (top)
Roni and Dalton at Boondocks photobooth - 2008 (bottom)

4

Can I Be On Your Schedule?

The first four years of Dalton's life were madness for us. Both John and I were working 70+ hours a week, and then coming home to a sick kid who always seemed to have a cold, dual ear infections, RSV (respiratory syncytial virus), pneumonia, or all of them at once. I spent so many hours at the doctors' office being reminded by a doctor with five kids and a stay-at-home wife, "If you stayed home full-time, your child would not be sick." Coming from a male doctor, I just took that as proof that I should work harder in all aspects of my life to prove him wrong. Girl power!

As a business owner and a one-woman-show, I found it difficult to set aside time to be with Dalton. I was constantly striving to be the best in my business, for fear that if I weren't there every time a client called, they would use someone else, and my business would go down in flames. If that happened, how would we pay for our life and all of our stuff? Yes, my priorities were way out of whack.

Little did I know, my son needed me more than ever. We were asked to leave by two daycares in his first four years because he was biting other kids and crying hysterically anytime I would drop him off. You'd have thought I'd have gotten the hint a bit sooner than four years into parenting, but I didn't. I am ashamed to say that my work took priority back then.

The summer that Dalton was 4, we built our house, and I finally moved into my home office thinking I could take care of him and work at the same time. It actually worked out pretty well for a while. He had his own desk and did his "work" while I did mine, but I often got engrossed in my work and let him play by himself for too long. I still beat myself up about this, but I soothe myself with the fact that it helped him become quite independent - keeping himself busy with drawing, coloring, Legos®, and cars. This actually served him quite well in the years to come.

One day during the summer after kindergarten, Dalton came into my office and asked me, "Can I be on your schedule today please?" Wow! Talk about a slap in the face! It was *that* day, right at *that* moment, that Dalton and I began to plan my calendar *together* each day to include at least one hour of completely uninterrupted Dalton-and-Mommy-time to do with *as he pleased*. We played Legos®, colored, made crafts, played games, grew amethysts and other rocks, went out for pizza, went to the park, went to the library, read tons of books, learned how to ride skateboards, went roller skating, went on bike rides, etc. Soon, those one-hour time frames turned into a couple hours, and sometimes they ended up being all afternoon. We made some awesome memories, and, for the most part, we had those special times every day that summer, and every summer after that, until his friends took precedence over me in his teen years. That's when *I* had to ask if *I* could be on *his* calendar. After he got a girlfriend, he was not *nearly* as accommodating as I had been. Imagine that!

During school, I attended every single field trip and class party/activity except two, and I'm pretty proud of that. Yet taking that time off during the day, meant I had to make up for it somewhere else. That was usually between 10pm and 4am. Needless to say, I didn't sleep a lot, and I was always exhausted, but Dalton always knew that his mom would do anything for him, and I have no regrets in that area.

My husband, John, however, will tell you that he has many regrets, the kind that constantly gnaw at him. John rarely attended daytime school functions, as he worked for a company that didn't allow time off very often. Additionally, when he was at home, he had tons of projects going on in the yard and garage that required his full attention, meaning lots of time away from Dalton and me. I would give John grief about it all the time. He either needed to forget about those projects or teach Dalton and I how to help him, so we could all be doing the projects together. For my perfectionist husband, that was a tough request. He would tell me that it took too much time to teach us or that he would get it done quicker without our help or that we wouldn't do it as well as he could. John wishes now that he had taken the time to include us.

Straightforward Tips for Parenting at Your Best

There's no special formula for parenting, yet there are several trains of thought regarding time management, fitting the most in your schedule to acquire the highest profit, be that money and/or time. I would recommend *all* parents and kids take classes and read books on time management to figure out a system that works best for each person as everyone's version of time management is different. Start your kids on this early, *before kindergarten* so they're not surprised by classroom schedules and early wake-up times. Plan vacations and family time first and work everything else around that.

Schedule cuddle time. Allow time for mishaps and spur-of-the-moment discussions. Have the patience to listen to your child's music and give them well-thought-out answers when they ask you what the words in your music mean. Sing together. Live in the moment. Cherish every second you have.

I've also found that the busiest people always seem to find time to fit in just one more thing and do it well. On the other hand, I know many folks that are not working or parenting who can't even keep their house clean, much less do laundry and get food on the table for dinner. It's all in how effectively one manages their time. Busy is good! It keeps your brain active and fresh and doesn't allow you the time to sit around and get lazy. Another great benefit of being busy is that it keeps everyone out of trouble.

Demanding schedules don't always consist of sports, work, and chores. In fact, a lot of busyness can be playing games with your family, going to concerts and sporting events, vacationing, camping, and enjoying hobbies together - anything that keeps you *actively together* making memories.

We *all* have the ability to fit whatever it is we want to do into our schedules, including sleep, exercise, and eating healthy. The trick is learning *what is important enough* to add to the schedule. Everyone's priorities are different, and we all make choices to live with the rewards and consequences of our scheduling selections, whatever those may be. Choose wisely, and be very open to change, as life's dramas always seem to pop up when we have the most on our plates.

When is it a convenient time to deal with the unexpected? Never. Just be open to change. From experience, I can attest that some of the best conversations and memories happen when the engine blows in your truck 1100 miles away from home, or your kid misses the bus, or they break their arm in gym class while you're in the middle of a meeting. Many gifts can also come from fear and loss such as breaking your wrist and ribs, having surgery to get it all put back together, and then finding out the company where you've worked for the last ten years is going out of business. You end up on a path that leads you to your own business and more quality time with your kid. While I don't wish these same

> *I do wish you enough misfortunes that you learn what having fortune really is.*

mishaps on you, *I do wish you enough misfortunes that you learn what having fortune really is.*

Moreover, as John and I move through the grieving process, being busy helps us get through each day, so we plan our days to fit in as much as possible, leaving very little downtime. Downtime allows very dark thoughts to come into our heads, and while it may not be the healthiest thing for us to do all the time, being busy is the safest avenue on our journey right now. Subsequently, we are exhausted at bedtime, and we are motivated to get up each morning by the fact that we have clients depending on us to do our jobs effectively. I'm deducing this same idea may work well for those going through job loss, divorce, and addiction as well.

> Song: The Dollar
> Written and Performed by Jamey Johnson

JRD - Dalton, Nebraska - 9/6/2004

5

Real Life Business Card

When Dalton was in elementary school, he and I sat down one day and decided to write down our job titles and discuss who we were. I think this was a school project, but I can't remember for sure. Either way, it was a real turning point for me.

I chose to put mine in order from birth forward so I could figure them out. Mine was typed on the computer while Dalton sat at his desk and wrote his on a piece of green colored paper.

I typed, "I came into this world as Ron and Denise's daughter, which also made me a granddaughter, a great-granddaughter, a niece, and a cousin. Then, as time moved forward, I became a sister to Shauna, a neighbor, a friend to many, and a girlfriend to some. I am a student, a volunteer, an employee, John's wife, a daughter-in-law, a sister-in-law, an auntie, a business owner, and now I'm the most important person I'll ever be ... I'm your mommy."

Dalton's said something like, "Son, grandkid, nephew, cousin, student, friend," and something really funny that I can't remember now about his chores and being my slave. I just remember the two of us laughing for a long time about it when we shared what we wrote. (I would give anything to find the sheet of paper he wrote on that day!!!)

> *I'm the most important person I'll ever be ... I'm your mommy."*

Straightforward Tips for Parenting at Your Best

Take the time to write down your roles in life, then put them in order of importance, and allocate your time accordingly. Granted, working takes up a ton of time, but there are other sacrifices that can be made to spend more time and effort with the people you love most.

That lesson alone taught me that I am *far more* than just a business owner. In fact, while work is where I spend at least 1/3 of my time, it is *not* the most important place to spend my time. Knowing how to separate the two has always been a real struggle for me. I hope you make better choices than I did.

> Song: Count On Me
> Written by Bruno Mars, Philip Lawrence, and Ari Levine
> Performed by Bruno Mars

Dalton and John calmly discussing his meltdown at my sister's wedding - 5/10/2003

6

Speak UP!

No, not louder. It's about using the power of words to be positive with our children and everyone else around us.

For years, I worked for my mom. One day I had written a note on bright red paper to one of our investors, and I used the words, "DON'T FORGET..." in caps on the note. My mom said, "How about using 'Please remember' instead of 'DON'T FORGET' and using a lighter shade of paper; maybe a pastel color?"

That has always stuck with me, so I was diligent with Dalton in saying, "Please remember to..." instead of "Don't forget to..." as it has a much more positive spin to it.

Additionally, when he did something well, John and I were very conscious about commending him for a job well done, and when he didn't do so well, we tried our best to point out the negative first and end our comments with something positive. If nothing positive could be said about what he said or did, we reminded him that everyone makes mistakes and that we still loved him, yet we'd really appreciate it if he tried harder next time for a better outcome. Because Dalton was someone who really cared about other people's feelings, often putting their feelings before his own, we would ask him, "How do you think that made [name] feel?" More times than not, that question alone would make him rethink his actions enough to turn things around next time. Sometimes, it even prompted him into writing an apology note to that person on his own accord.

> *Instead of saying, "Don't forget," say, "Please remember."*

Straightforward Tips for Parenting at Your Best

Instead of saying, "Don't forget," say, "Please remember."
    Instead of asking, "How was your day," ask, "What was the best thing about your day?" or "What was your high

today?" It reduces the possibility of one-word answers and allows you to delve in further into their lives.

When raising your voice, let it be for great things like congratulating them on a job well done, rather than screaming at them for something that they won't hear anyway. This is one area in which I failed miserably. I habitually raised my voice at the wrong times with Dalton. More often than not, with both of our strong personalities, we would either end up in a yelling match, or he would simply sit and pretend to listen to me then go to his room, thankful to be done with my insanity. In very few of those instances did what I say mean anything to him because the instant I began yelling, he tuned me out.

There's nine simple steps I've learned since losing Dalton that seem to help me a lot with my emotions and anxiety. I think they can also help parents when things are ready to explode with their kids:

1. Look around.
2. Take a deep breath through your nose and let it all the way out through your mouth.
3. Find five things you can see.
4. Find four things you can touch.
5. Find three things you can hear.
6. Find two things you can smell.
7. Find one thing you can taste.

8. Take another deep breath through your nose and let it all the way out through your mouth.
9. Then take action.

In the time it takes you to do all of these things, the anger and anxiety have, hopefully, subsided enough that you can effectively handle the situation. If not, take a step back and let your child know you need to calm down before you discuss the current situation with them any further. Not only will it help you calm down, but it will also show them how to effectively manage their own anger. Teaching by example works best.

When you speak with them, do your best to list the items they need to improve on first and list the things they do/did well last, so you are leaving them with a positive thought.

> Song: Little Hercules
> Written by Craig D. Carothers
> Performed by Trisha Yearwood

Dalton with Mrs. Phelan,
the first teacher who he felt really cared about him
because she listened and she always spoke calmly.
5th Grade Graduation - 5/2009

Do You Hear What I Hear?

From the time we bring them into this world, our children are trying to communicate with us. With the first cry, the first smile, the first giggle, the first time they tell us "No!" and every breath in between, they want us to see and hear them and simply acknowledge their existence. Often times, we hear them speak and, before we've even listened to their complete thought, we begin coming up with a solution, cure, or a teaching moment, when all we really need to do is listen to them and really hear what they have to say.

Even though we may think what they are saying or doing is unimportant because it has to do with something minor like coloring a picture or someone taking their toy when they have ten others to play with, we need to remember that those things *are* what's important in their lives right at that particular moment. They don't always need our advice. In fact, more often than not, they just need to be heard. If we actually take the extra few minutes to stop and listen, we may find that just letting them tell us what's on their mind allows them to work through it themselves.

I was a pro at coming up with a solution before Dalton ever stopped talking. He would get so frustrated with me that he'd stomp off before I was finished giving him my advice. I'm sure you can imagine the frustration this caused between us. He'd be mad that I didn't listen all the way through, and I'd be mad that he didn't want to hear my brilliant Motherly advice.

> Just letting them tell us what's on their mind allows them to work through it themselves.

Straightforward Tips for Parenting at Your Best

Stop and listen until they are completely finished with their thought and ask yourself, "Are they asking me a question, or are they just asking to be heard?" Then acknowledge what they said by summarizing their words back to them ("If I understood you correctly, you said..."). Stop to help them at that moment, or if you're in the middle of something else, actively schedule a time with them to handle the issue within a short period of time. (When he was little, Dalton told me "a short period of time to a kid is less than 30 minutes." I'm sure he had no idea how much time that really was, but he knew it felt like a long time.)

Song: Watching You
Written by Rodney Atkins, Steve Dean, and Brian Gene White
Performed by Rodney Atkins

Noah, Sam, Nic, Dalton 3/2013 (top) / Nico and Dalton - 10/2013 (bottom)

I've Got a Feeling

We spent a lot of time teaching Dalton to surround himself with great people by setting an example. By doing so, we also taught him to trust his own instincts. In teaching him to reach out and make new friends, he learned what kinds of people he did and did not like to be around.

One night, he was telling me the day's highs and lows. His low that day was that he had met a girl who was very sad. Her mother had recently passed away, and she felt like her father didn't want her around anymore. We discussed how important it was that he be there to listen to her, and we discussed other ways he could help her. We also discussed that maybe his "high" for the day was the same as his "low," because it was a blessing that he could be a friend to this girl.

Over the next couple of weeks, I asked how his friend was doing, and he said she seemed better, but that he was a little concerned; maybe she was "better than she should be." As it turned out, she had been asking Dalton for money saying her dad wouldn't give her lunch money. After forfeiting his own lunch for several days, he saw her talking to a known troublemaker at school and watched her hand him $20 (the lunch money Dalton had given her). The troublemaker handed her something back. Dalton immediately approached her asking what she gave that guy money for, and she said it was for a pill to help her study. Obviously, his gut feeling was right, and he told her that he could no longer be her friend. It was a good lesson for him to realize that he had boundaries, and they weren't boundaries we had given him. (We also let her counselor know so they could get her some help.)

> It was a good lesson for him to realize that he had boundaries, and they weren't boundaries we had given him.

Straightforward Tips for Parenting at Your Best

Help your child find comfort in people and things they care about, and also discuss the characteristics of people and things they want to avoid. Doing this in writing and revisiting it at the beginning of every school semester is very helpful. In setting those parameters up front, while they are still young, it will help them build insight as to what fulfills their wants and needs, and what doesn't. Thus, they can make better choices when you're not right there to help.

It's also good to discuss finding a happy place, a place where they feel safe when life is getting to them. This could be their bedroom, a friend's house, the park, anywhere. It's also important that you know where their happy place is. Having somewhere to go when they feel like they need a little time to themselves allows them the opportunity to work through situations and thoughts on their own.

> Song: Heart To Heart (Stelen's Song)
> Written and Performed by Toby Keith

Dalton and David Behr at Competitive Edge Seminar - 12/3/2008

9

Something to Believe In

Children, especially teenagers, will often listen to ideas from other trusted adults before they take advice from their own parents. From the age of 7, when Dalton was old enough to sit still for long periods of time, I took him to seminars on everything from sales to customer service, goal setting, and time management. We also went to inspirational seminars like *How High Can You Bounce* with Roger Crawford (he loved that one!). We always sat in the front row so as not to be distracted by other attendees, and he always brought a pen and notebook so he could take notes just like I did.

At the Roger Crawford seminar in 2008, we had to write down our most significant accomplishments, as well as what we wanted financially, career-wise, and personally within the next 10 years. It was really neat to watch his 10-year-old mind work so diligently on his answers. Once he was done, the host, David Behr, brought him up on stage and gave him $20 toward his goal of owning a Ferrari by age 20. The list and the $20 are still hanging on his wall. It was something he looked at every single day, along with the list of his goals he wrote at age 10...

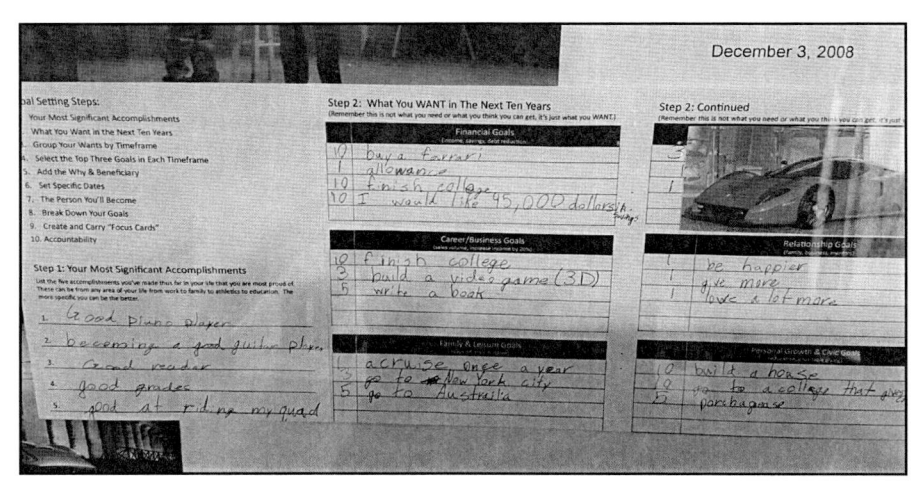

All of us need something to believe in, be it religion, politics, love, family, a cause close to our hearts, etc.

One thing I'm very proud of in our parenting of Dalton was that we never required him to choose a specific religion. He went with several friends and family members to their churches and clubs and made decisions for himself about what he believed. We never forced our beliefs upon him, yet we always kept the lines of communication open about where he was going, who he was going with, and what the plan was for activities. Afterward, we would always talk about what they ended up doing, what was discussed, what he learned, and how he felt about it.

The same stood true for politics. My husband is pretty right wing, and I'm pretty in-the-middle, and our extended family is all over the place. When we discuss politics around here, we always discuss the reasons we feel the way we do, so that we all have the opportunity to at least try to understand the opposing view. Apparently, Dalton learned a lot from our conversations; as we later learned, he was usually the "referee" when talks between friends got out of hand.

> *Give them the opportunity to make their own decisions and mistakes while they're young, while it doesn't cost anything.*

While we wanted him to have something to believe in, we also wanted his mind to be open to the possibilities of taking what he liked and discarding what he didn't, so he could form his own beliefs in all aspects of his life. It helped him become very mature for his age.

Straightforward Tips for Parenting at Your Best

It is our job as parents to give our children all the opportunities we can and then let them make choices *without* our influence. Allowing our children to choose small things like food and what color crayon to use when they are toddlers, helps give them confidence at a young age to know they can make their own decisions, thus allowing them the confidence as they mature to choose good friends (something Dalton did very well). It also allows them the ability to learn how to study, work, save, budget, and spend their own money effectively. This can also be said for choosing beliefs in religion and politics and every other small or large decision in their lives. How else can we expect them to make educated decisions as college students and adults, if we don't give them the opportunity to make their own decisions and mistakes while they're young, while it doesn't cost anything?

Know when to step away and allow them to make their own mistakes. Start with the small stuff, and the big stuff will work itself out.

> Song: I Hope You Dance
> Written by Mark Sanders and Tia Sillers
> Performed by Lee Ann Womack

Dax and Dalton - 2012

10

My Home Is Your Home Is Our Home; We're in This Together

As parents, it's important to teach our children that we are in this life together. That means we all work toward our goals together, as a team, so that we can all have rights to the end result. Since kids these days are feeling more entitled, more anxious, and lazier than ever before, we as a society need to teach them what it means to take ownership of their lives and teach them step-by-step how to figure out what it is they want to live for and how to obtain it.

I remember my mom telling me as a teenager that the house we lived in was her house. It went something like this, "You live in MY HOUSE! You will abide by MY

RULES! And you WILL do the chores I require to live here." My first thought was, "Well, if this is your house, then I'll leave, and you can do the chores yourself." Did that happen? No. Of course not. I did the chores required and, at the time, I was mad at my mom for making me do them. Am I saying she was wrong to make me do chores? Absolutely not. I certainly grew up knowing how to keep a clean house, and I thank her for that along with the million other lessons she taught me. "Thanks, Mom."

That said, one of my goals when I had my own family, was to make sure my family knew that the house we lived in was "our house." I was just sure that knowing it was "ours" would entice everyone into helping anytime it was needed, without argument. That wasn't always the case, and we often argued about getting the trash bags into the trash cans after they had been emptied. Nonetheless, I do feel like Dalton was a whole lot better sport than I was at his age about cleaning bathrooms and floors and emptying trash, knowing this was also his house, and he wasn't just a guest in it.

From the age of 4, Dalton did chores like emptying trash, putting trash bags in trash cans, dusting, and cleaning his own bathroom (with help, of course). He also gathered hangers and sorted clothes (I still have the signs on the wall in the laundry room showing him what items go in which hamper to be washed). As he grew, his responsibilities did too, like feeding the dogs, emptying the dishwasher, vacuuming, mowing the yard, cleaning up dog poop, etc. He always had a chore chart where he could learn to mark what he had done and earn some money for his efforts. (Example of Dalton's Chore Chart here: http://wp.me/a4n6Er-1m.)

I looked at this as teaching him to do a job and then complete his time sheet to get paid, just like it would be in the business world. If he didn't turn in his time sheet, he didn't get paid. While we never had the opportunity to have this tested when he turned 16 and got a real job, I do believe he would have been a stellar employee, because we taught him early how to work and also how to ask for payment.

Straightforward Tips for Parenting at Your Best

Remember that you are in this together. Come up with ways you can prove that by making meal plans and grocery lists and shopping together, as well as planning and saving for vacations together, and budgeting together. There's something to be said for kids who know how much it costs to run a household – mortgage, groceries, cars, fuel, etc. and how many hours you have to work to provide these things. Share your highs and lows, do chores together, and share your dreams for the future, etc.

In the chore chart, you will notice that I never listed cleaning his room as a chore, as I felt that was his own space, and he had to live in it (with the door shut, if needed). Additionally, I never entered his room unless I was invited because that was his space. Even if he was mad at me, I would knock on the door and ask if I could come in. I was always invited.

As I think back on things, Dalton was involved in nearly everything we did.

When Dalton was small, each time we were planning a vacation I made it a point that we had a see-through jar on the counter, so when any of us had any extra change, we tossed it in the jar. Then, when we went on our trip, it was a big deal when we did something he really enjoyed that we used the money we all raised together to make it happen. In all reality, the change in the jar barely covered anything, but it always helped him feel like he had a special part in making it happen and he was proud of that.

Over the years, we purchased a few run down homes to fix up and sell, and Dalton was there with us every night after school, either doing homework or helping us paint, tile, clean, sweep, etc. He hated those months when we were turning homes, but he learned a lot and was always very happy when one sold, and we celebrated at an arcade or amusement park of his choosing.

Another tip that I cannot take credit for, I learned in a budgeting class many years ago...

Most kids want a soda or lemonade when they go to a restaurant. We always gave Dalton the option to either have the drink or choose water instead and get the money for the drink. Most often, he chose the money. The key was that we had the coins right there with us so he could get an immediate reward for making a healthier choice, both physically and financially. He kept that money separate from his other earnings for a long time and eventually used it to buy a video game. This is a great tool that I am so thankful to have learned long ago. We could learn a lot from this small lesson as adults too... *Starbucks, anyone?*

> There's something to be said for kids who know how much it costs to run a household.

As a mom and a REALTOR®, I would also recommend that you include your children when you are planning a move. Other real estate agents may want to wring my neck for saying this, but it's important that children feel involved and that their thoughts are included when searching for a home. Granted, it's not always important to take them with you for every single showing, but once you've narrowed it down to two or three options, it's important to take them to see the homes you are considering. Then, sit down and have everyone weigh the pros and cons of each property together. How much do they cost? How much will you spend on a monthly basis, and how much time will you have to spend working and traveling to and from work? How much effort it will take to keep it clean, etc.? It's important they know their feelings do count, and it's also important they know the financial commitments. I've been in both situations with buyers, where they've included kids and not included kids. The clients who included their kids had a much better transition into the new home and schools than the clients who made the entire decision without including their kids.

I would also recommend writing a Family Business Plan together so that each member of the family knows what they are responsible for on a daily basis; this includes chores and homework, yet it also includes emotional responsibilities as well, like supporting each other and taking the time to listen and care. Here's an example of ours...

Lambrecht Family Business Plan

*Our mission is to be devoted to living
our lives as a loving and respectful family.
We will work together to strengthen our community
through our active involvement in meaningful
activities and charities.
We will set strong examples for Dalton,
extended family, friends, and neighbors.
We will raise Dalton with the proper amounts
of nurturing and discipline.
We are committed to always considering each others' feelings
and putting our family's needs above our own.
We are thankful each day that we can be together.*

Expectations of John:
- ♥ *Provide support and love to Roni and Dalton.*
- ♥ *Work diligently to provide money to pay bills, have nice things, and take vacations.*
- ♥ *Take care of the yard and exterior of house.*
- ♥ *Maintain and repair house and vehicles as needed.*
- ♥ *Laundry.*
- ♥ *Help Dalton with homework as needed.*

Expectations of Roni:
- ♥ *Provide support and love to John and Dalton.*

- *Provide good, healthy food to feed our family.*
- *Work diligently to provide money to pay bills, have nice things, and take vacations.*
- *Keep house clean.*
- *Maintain and repair house and vehicles as needed.*
- *Laundry.*
- *Help Dalton with homework as needed.*
- *Volunteer at school and attend all school functions.*

Expectations of Dalton:
- *Provide support and love to Mom and Dad.*
- *Do well in school – 3.2GPA or above is acceptable.*
- *Practice guitar 30 minutes per day (2-15 minute sessions), 4 days per week + lesson.*
- *Practice piano 30 minutes per week (2-15 minute sessions).*
- *Pick up after yourself.*
- *Offer to help Dad or Mom before playing.*
- *Help Mom and Dad maintain and repair house and vehicles as needed.*
- *Do chores from chore sheet each day without being told.*
- *Keep track of chores for allowance and turn in weekly for payment.*

John's Goals:
- *See Mom at least four times per year.*

- ♥ Own my own business.

Roni's Goals:
- ♥ Become an independent brokerage.
- ♥ Meet and write songs with songwriters.
- ♥ Write a book.

Dalton's Goals:
- ♥ Be an actor.
- ♥ Write a book.
- ♥ Become a sniper in the Marines.

Family Goals:
- ♥ Go on vacation to Australia.

Granted, this plan could use some major upgrading, but it helped us along our journey. It hung on our refrigerator so we could all see it every day, and we often discussed it and made modifications as goals were met or life changes occurred.

Song: Sowin' Love
Written by Paul Overstreet and Don Schlitz
Performed by Paul Overstreet

JRD - Glamis - 3/2012 (top)
Dalton's cousin, Bella-Boo and her Dal-too 12/2006 (bottom)

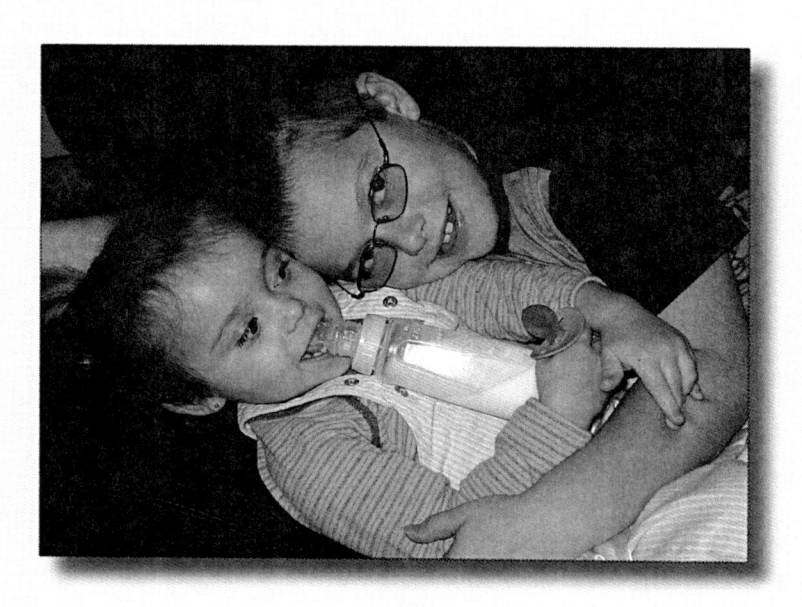

11

Get Real!

Something I have learned to do quite well is to apologize. In fact, Dalton was very good at it too. We may have gotten a little hot-headed at times, but we always knew when we were at fault (after we thought about it, of course) and we always apologized when that was the case.

I often reminded Dalton that it was my first time being a mom, just like it was his first time being a kid. I was honest in letting him know when I made mistakes with him and in other areas of my life. It's important that our children keep us on the same playing field as they're on, meaning I'm no better than him, or anyone else, and I do not deserve to be put on a pedestal any more than the next person.

When I did make a mistake with Dalton, I would explain to him that his feelings do matter, and we would discuss how to avoid the same argument in the future. All said, though, he always knew that I was the mom and what I said was the way it was going to go.

One evening, I was preparing to speak to a large class of peers on a topic I was passionate about. I was really nervous, and Dalton could feel it as I was very short with him. He asked me to stop what I was doing and talk to him. I explained to him that I was teaching a class the next day, and I was very nervous about speaking and worried about how I would sound. It was so funny - like he was the parent, and I was the kid.

> *All children are far smarter than we give them credit for.*

He asked me to present the topic to him in our living room while he sat on the couch and watched me. Funny enough, it helped. And I did a pretty good job the next day too!

There were so many great learning experiences here...

- ♥ For me: I was short with Dalton when I had no right to be, and he called me on it. He listened to me speak and told me what he thought I could improve on. It opened my eyes to the magic of listening to a child's ideas; even though he had no idea what I was talking about, he could look at the big picture and give me good pointers. All children are far smarter than we give them credit for.
- ♥ For him: He knew I was being short with him and called me on it. He learned that I'm not just his mom; I'm a professional too. He learned that his advice was worth listening to, and it boosted his confidence. He also knew that what I was speaking about was "wayyyy boring!"

Mostly, though, it taught me that even a young child can care deeply about you and your feelings, and allowing him to help me helped both of us in many different ways.

Straightforward Tips for Parenting at Your Best

If you make a mistake by saying or doing the wrong thing, be sure to apologize. We're all human, and we all make mistakes. Just be honest about it. Remember, every child is different, so whether you have an only child, or you have nineteen, personalities and circumstances still make you a first-time parent to each child.

> *We need to teach our kids compassion for themselves and for others, and that starts at home.*

Also, it's okay to let our kids know when we're struggling with things outside of parenting. I'm not saying that we put our problems on them and worry them, but rather share with our children that we have daily struggles just like they do. Too many kids think this world revolves completely around them, and that's just not true. We need to teach our kids compassion for themselves and for others, and that starts at home.

> Song: Humble and Kind
> Written by Lori McKenna
> Performed by Tim McGraw

Dalton's 3rd Birthday learning how to ride a bike - 4/25/2001

12

Follow Through

In life, especially in parenting, one of the largest obstacles we face is following through on what we say we're going to do. There are an unlimited number of excuses ... life is too busy, we're too tired to deal with it, we think it's not important right now, etc. One of the most important virtues we can teach our children is that our word matters, and that means we must follow through with what we say we're going to do.

Here's an example:

You and your teenager are up at 6am getting ready for school and work. Ten minutes before you're ready to leave to catch the bus, your teenager remembers they forgot to finish their homework last night, and they have a dramatic teenage meltdown. After you have calmed them and taken a few minutes to review the homework they missed, they have now missed the bus. This means you have to take them all the way to school (fourteen miles round trip), which is in the opposite direction you needed to go to get to your meeting on time. Resolving in your mind that you'll now be late for the meeting and contacting the appropriate parties to let them know, you've let your teenager know you'll drive them to school and that they can finish their homework in the car. All of this has thrown your entire day off track and made you late for every back-to-back meeting all day long.

You walk in the door at 6pm and see unfinished food on the kitchen counter, a coat on the floor, shoes that should be by the door in two different places, and your teenager is playing a video game instead of tending to

> *Our word matters, and that means we must follow through with what we say we're going to do.*

the homework in front of them on the coffee table. Can you feel the explosion about to happen? I can hear it now, "After everything we went through this morning because you forgot to do your homework last night, and I come home to this?!?!?!" The rest is not pretty at all.

The last time this happened, you swore you'd take the video game away. But you're tired, and you don't want to argue so you calm down and ask politely for your teenager to stop playing the game and get busy on their homework, only to receive the response that they are in the middle of the game and can't quit right now.

Ask yourself...
- ♥ Will they survive even if the game is ended right now? *Yes.*
- ♥ What message are you sending if you allow them to continue to play? *When my parents are tired, I can get away with anything.*

Parenting is not a job you just get to do when you're feeling fantastic. In fact, most of the time, you are exhausted. You signed up for this, for better, for worse. Do your job! Unplug the game. Take it away. Shut off the Wi-Fi. Do WHATEVER it takes to end the game NOW.

In a perfect world, your teenager would kindly oblige and get busy on their homework, but reality tells you that there's a fight brewing, and another explosion is about to happen. Tired or not, you're the parent, you make the rules, and homework comes before games.

Straightforward Tips for Parenting at Your Best

Teach your children early about rewards and consequences and stick to it. Rather than yelling at them for leaving their toys all over, choose a toy they love and explain to them that, if this happens again, that toy will go to another child who will appreciate it. Then, when it does happen again, donate the toy to a good cause. I mean that. You really do donate it (even if it cost you a lot of money). There is nothing more important in life than to teach your child that they must do what is required to get what they want.

This quote from Denzel Washington has been hanging in our house for many years...

"Do what you gotta do so you can do what you wanna do."

> Song: My Wish
> Written by Jeffrey Steele and Steve Robson
> Performed by Rascal Flatts

Dalton - Walden Sand Dunes - 7/2010

Use The Tools You Have Been Given

I used to preach, "Use the tools you have been given," to Dalton and his friends at least once a day, if not more; often enough that it became a big joke between all of us. The thought process here is that we are very blessed to have this life, the relationships within it, as well as all the tangible items we've either earned or been given. It would be disrespectful to us and to those who have bestowed those gifts upon us, not to use them to their full potential.

Here are some examples from our own experiences ...

♥ When our niece was about 3 years old, she wanted a toy. We were in the midst of remodeling a house, so we told her that every nail she picked up and put into a can was worth one penny. There were hundreds of nails, and she filled several coffee cans. This was a win-win for all of us. The nails all got picked up without a fight, we worked on counting together, and she ended up having enough to buy the toy she wanted all by herself, thus building confidence and skill.

♥ Dalton was trying to hang up a shelf in his room beating a nail into the wall with his shoe, knowing full well that he was given a real toolbox with actual tools in it for Christmas. I reminded him where his tools were and helped him find the tape measure, the hammer, and the level, and calmly taught him how to put that shelf up the right way. In doing so, I literally helped him find the right tools to complete the job.

♥ Dalton wanted to buy a video game that was coming out soon. Luckily, it had snowed, and there were a lot of neighbors around who needed someone to shovel. He knocked on doors, introduced himself, and offered to shovel driveways for a fair price. Four driveways later, he had helped out four neighbors, gotten some great exercise, and earned enough money to purchase that video game with his own hard-earned money. We gave him the idea. John gave him the shovel and helped out some with the 4-wheeler plow (the tools), and Dalton made it happen. Had he chosen not to, the video game would have remained on the shelf at the store until he found some ambition.

♥ Dalton had been begging me for a cell phone. He'd say things like, "Everybody else has one," "You know, Mom, I'm the only kid in the entire high school without a phone," "If I had a phone, you could reach me anytime you needed me." I was completely against it until the night I dropped him off at a movie and then found out he didn't go to a movie, but went bowling instead. To make a long story short, we couldn't find him for hours, and we nearly had heart failure. So, I won the battle of the constant connection until he was 15, and then he won. That said, he wanted it badly enough that he figured out who needed help in the neighborhood so he could come up with two months of payments up front, knowing if the payments for the following months were not received on the 20th of each month, the phone was taken away. That happened once because he didn't have quite enough money to pay the bill, but within a few days, he figured out that raking the leaves for the neighbor was a good thing. He made some money, paid me for two months' worth and got his phone back. Interestingly enough, right before we left for our trip to Glamis, Dalton had paid me for two months of his phone bill to cover January and February, and that's how long we left his phone on after he passed away.

> Other than love, support, food, water, and a place to call home, all they really need from us is to teach them how to become self-sufficient.

Straightforward Tips for Parenting at Your Best

Even when you refrain from buying them a toy, a phone, a car, etc., your kids will still know you love them. In fact, they will soon realize that other than love, support, food, water, and a place to call home, all they really need from us is to teach them how to become self-sufficient.

There are so many times in life when we must figure out a new way of making something good happen because the old ways aren't working anymore. Teaching our children to look outside the box and use their current set of circumstances to create better opportunities for their own future is something we must do early on so they can have that skill mastered by adulthood.

Teach your children what "tools" they have to work with and how to search out other "tools." These can be actual tools, like hammers and nails, and they can be figurative tools, such as learning a new skill, meeting new people, nurturing current relationships, offering to do a chore/job for pay, or volunteering. It may be using skills they already have to help someone (drawing, crafting, tutoring, driving, knowing how to assemble things, etc.). We all have an unlimited "toolbox" at our disposal. The key is knowing where to find those tools and how to use them effectively.

Song: Coat of Many Colors
Written and Performed by Dolly Parton

Dalton making sugar cookies at Grandma Wing's house - 12/2009

How Bad Do You Want It?

In teaching our children to use the tools they have been given, we are giving them the ability to make something out of nothing, and, more importantly, the confidence that they have the ability to do so. When we enable them by "giving in" or "breaking down," we are only teaching them to work just enough to wear us out, so we'll give in to their expectations. John and I see this in ourselves, our families, friends, and especially within our government.

As Thomas Jefferson said,
"A government big enough to give you everything you want, is strong enough to take everything you have."

In our children's lives, we are their government. Let's hope we do a better job of it than the real government does.

Life is exhausting. Sometimes it's just easier to give in instead of saying "no" and dealing with the disagreements that may ensue. We're all guilty of this, yet by doing so, we are creating a society that believes we are all entitled. The truth is nobody, children or adults alike, is ever going to lose out in life because they didn't get something they wanted. They can live without whatever it is until they want it badly enough to earn it.

> They can live without whatever it is until they want it badly enough to earn it.

I remember my 18th birthday when my mom wrote something in my birthday card to the effect of, "Happy Birthday! Now that you're 18, rent will be $200 per month beginning today." I was upset about it, but I paid rent every single month so I could have a place to live. Little did I know, my mom was teaching me how to budget effectively so that I could soon move out on my own and be able to afford it. She did her research and made sure that using the $200 rent would be the correct amount for getting out on my own. For nearly two years, I paid the rent each month and abided by her house rules. Much to my surprise, she saved every penny of that money and allowed me to use it toward the down payment on my first condo. Back then, my mortgage payment was $160, so the rest went toward utilities and other homeowner needs. These days, that number would be MUCH larger, yet I still recommend this practice, as it's exactly what we had planned to do for Dalton.

Straightforward Tips for Parenting at Your Best

One of the biggest tools we use in our society is money. Teaching our children at an early age how to use it effectively is a true gift. And while learning to manage money is equally as important as core subjects required in our school system, it is up to parents alone to teach children what it means to manage money effectively. In doing so, we must give our children the opportunity to fail while it is still relatively cheap to do so – before they are 18 and before their worlds are affected by credit reporting. This means that we need to start early. Age 4 was appropriate to start with our son.

Set a precedent for earning what they want, instead of

> *We must give our children the opportunity to fail while it is still relatively cheap to do so.*

expecting it. Teach your child about instant gratification and delayed gratification, as well as review how long the enthusiasm lasts after each one. There are several ways this can be done. Below is just one example.

You're at the store, and your child sees a $3.00 toy they think they need right this moment. Do you buy it? NO! Give them the opportunity to earn that toy on their own by letting them know there are some chores that you need help with at home that will help them meet their goal.

When you get home, write down:
Toy = $3.00
Tax = $0.26 (in a positive way, you'll need to explain what tax is and why it's needed)
Total = $3.26

Now, discuss with your child what they can do to earn this money. At age four, with guidance, they are perfectly capable of helping with the laundry by sorting clothes, gathering hangers from the low sections in the closet, folding, and sorting socks. Sometimes they will need the help of picture instructions. They can help with things like emptying and putting bags into small trash cans, dusting tables and chairs, helping set the table, helping empty the dishwasher, helping to dry dishes and many other things. You can even make up other jobs like having them take pictures of your furniture so you can give it to your insurance agent. Be creative. Most important, be patient with them as you teach them how to do each chore. Remember, this training will be ongoing. They will not learn or remember every step you teach them the first or second go-around. It takes repetition; often 15-20 times at that age.

Now get out another piece of paper and make a list of the chores you are willing to teach and pay for along with their values:

Sort clothes = .25
Gather hangers = .25
Sort socks = .25
Dust = .50
Empty trash = .25
Put bags in empty trash cans = .25

Remind them that they will be getting a lot of money while they work, and give them something special to carry their money in. The key here is instant gratification with the money, so make sure you have a lot of change on hand so you can pay them right away for their completed chores. That keeps them excited about the money and helping you. Within a week, they'll have enough money to buy the toy.

When they have earned enough money, make it an event. Go back to the store. Help them find the toy. Allow them to make the purchase themselves while you watch and help only as needed. (Often, if you tell the store clerk what's happening, they will be very helpful in cheering your child on too - you can even write the clerk a note before you get to the store and hand it to them before you check out.)

Plan to do this each time your child wants something and they will learn to work for what they want instead of expecting a handout.

There's a brilliant book and website to help teach your tween/teenager how to manage money effectively. Written by my friend, Craig Kaley, his website and book are called *Money Athletics*, and I highly recommend his strategy to ALL parents. It's close to the strategy we used with Dalton, but much more detailed.

Another tip for our kids (and anyone looking to be great in their field of interest) is to locate and offer to work for suppliers/vendors in their field of interest for *free* for a week as time allows (think of it as a longer and more detailed version of *Take Your Child to Work Day*). The amount of inside information one can gain from this is incredible. Not only does it increase knowledge within their field of interest, it also increases awareness in their industry that they are willing to go above and beyond to learn new things. It can also create opportunities for growth on both sides (employer/employee or supplier/vendor) knowing why things are done the way they are, and each party can improve their own tasks knowing how it will help the other side. Additionally, when layoffs occur, it prepares them for entrance into other facets of their field.

An example of this is when I first started in the real estate industry as a loan closer. I decided it would be a good opportunity to offer my help to the title companies for *free* for a week at a time when my business was slow. This gave me insight into how and why their procedures were the way they were, and it gave me some great ideas as to how I could help them with the transactions I did with them. Furthermore, when my business was slow after the 2008 crash, I always had work available when I needed it because I had made so many friends in the industry.

It's all a matter of asking, "How bad do you want it?" and then helping them learn the steps it takes to get there.

As the accomplished Warren Buffett once said,
"Give your children enough to do something,
but not enough to do nothing."

> Song: Where Does the Money Come From
> Written by Kevin Fisher and Fred Wilhelm
> Performed by Tonic Sol-Fa

Dalton with Grandpa and Grandma Wing - New York 3/2009 (top)
Dalton with Grandma Jean - Texas 10/2004 (bottom)

Respect – Bring It Back!

In a world where we're always "plugged in" and "connected," it seems like there's less personal connection than ever, and with less personal connection comes less respect. Manners are the first thing to go. Using "please" and "thank you," and "yes ma'am" and "yes sir," seem to be a thing of the past. Bring them back!

As an adult, we are the true measurement for our kids when it comes to respect. Ask yourself, "Do I use 'please' and 'thank you' with our family, friends, and strangers? When my meal comes out incorrectly at a restaurant, do I flip out at the waiter and demean them, or do I kindly ask for a new meal? When a teacher makes a mistake with my child, do I give them the opportunity to correct their mistake, or do I immediately get administration involved and scream at them for their lack of professionalism?"

Moreover, when commenting on how others look or act in front of our children, we are teaching them how to be judgmental. Be it a neighbor, the janitor, a waitress, teacher, high-powered executive, or the President, each of these people should be treated equally and fairly, and we should not be the ones judging them.

> *In any situation where our kids are with us, they are watching how we handle ourselves.*

Straightforward Tips for Parenting at Your Best

In any situation where our kids are with us, they are watching how we handle ourselves, and while we don't always remember that fact, we should always treat others with the utmost respect, free of judgment. If it comes naturally, then we never have to worry if our kids are watching. Practice makes perfect! (Or at least close to perfect.)

Additionally, if our kids see us using phrases such as "please" and "thank you" and opening doors for others, or allowing someone to go in front of us in a line, they will also learn to do these things.

One way we were very careful about this with Dalton was by making sure that we always complimented others for a job well done in front of him so he could see how kindness affects others first-hand.

> Song: Nothin' Grows In Shadows
> Written by Rhett Akins, Dallas Davidson, and Doug Johnson
> Performed by Jake Owen

Dalton's 12th birthday at Chili's - 4/25/2010

Daily Rituals and Traditions

One of our regular practices on Sundays was folding laundry. We have a huge, purple bin that's nearly three times the size of a normal laundry basket. Once all of our hang-up laundry is done, the rest goes in the bin, and it gets really full (it used to anyway). Dalton and I would take it in the bedroom and dump it on the top of the bed. Then Dalton would climb up on the bed behind the pile and start sorting socks into piles - his, mine, and John's. Along the way, I'd be making piles of my underwear and one big pile of John and Dalton's underwear for Dalton to sort (they wore the same size and I could never tell them apart, but Dalton sure could). I'd put everything away while throwing socks at Dalton to add to his pile. (Yes, *at* him, not *to* him. We always made a game of it.) Then, when I was done with my portion of the laundry, we'd finish sorting socks together and put them all away.

This entire chore would usually take us about 45 minutes to complete, and it was something we'd done nearly every week together since he was a toddler (it's great for teaching them to concentrate and match things up). The best part was that we'd talk the whole time and usually, by the time we were done, I'd crawl up on the bed with him, and we'd talk for another hour or two. This is one of my very favorite memories with Dalton; something I wouldn't trade for anything in the world. So go fold some laundry with your kids; you wouldn't believe some of the stories they tell you!

> Go fold some laundry with your kids; you wouldn't believe some of the stories they tell you!

Straightforward Tips for Parenting at Your Best

Think of rituals and traditions as little daily or weekly occurrences; not huge, organized, overly-planned events. Think of them as the sayings you have when you tell each other goodbye before school and work, how and when your kids hug you, or holding hands and singing in the car as you drive them places. Recall the funny jokes that you tell each other over and over, wearing specific clothes to cheer on your favorite team, and how they tie their shoes (or how they leave them untied and drive you crazy). Reminisce about how they wrap themselves up in their blankets and pillows, how they smile that funny smile every time you try to take a picture of them, that special look you have to communicate something specific, etc. There are so many small events that just happen in our normal way of life, and they are *far* more special than the big events. Cherish them and write about them in your journal.

Song: It Won't Be Like This For Long
Written by Darius Rucker,
Chris DuBois, and Ashley Gorley
Performed by Darius Rucker

Dalton's 15th birthday - 4/25/2013

Dalton's 15th Birthday party playing airsoft
and then coming home to hang out with his best friends.

Celebrate!

There are so many ways to celebrate our children, and the most important way to do that is to give them our time and attention.

Straightforward Tips for Parenting at Your Best

Praise them for things they've done well, even as simple as remembering to hang up their coat or putting their backpack away.

Inexpensive ways to celebrate your child could include:
- ♥ Verbally telling them you're proud of them (doing this in front of others is always good too).
- ♥ Writing them a quick love letter for their lunchbox or backpack that they'll find unexpectedly.
- ♥ Sending them an appreciative text.
- ♥ Sitting down with them and listening to their stories.
- ♥ Journaling with them or writing a story together.
- ♥ Going to the library.
- ♥ Reading a series of novels together in which the characters age with your child - our favorite was the Sammy Keyes series by Wendelin Van Draanen. We started when Dalton was in 4th grade and read 17 of the 18 books together. I read the last one myself after he passed away. Other great series include Harry Potter, Nancy Drew, Hardy Boys, 39 Clues, Guardians of ga'Hoole, Diary of a Wimpy Kid, and Little House On the Prairie. Ask your librarian where to begin; there are many more.
- ♥ Libraries often have authors in for book signings and seminars, and it can be a great reward to get a signed book from their favorite author.
- ♥ Dance together.

- ♥ Letting them choose what's for dinner.
- ♥ Cooking or baking together.
- ♥ Doing an art project together.
- ♥ Playing a sport together.
- ♥ Playing a game together. (Dalton loved Speed, Uno®, and Sequence®.)
- ♥ Going to the science store and finding a creative project like growing amethysts or building volcanoes, etc.
- ♥ Camping.
- ♥ Fishing.
- ♥ Allowing them to choose the next movie and/or dinner out.
- ♥ Making a bulletin board of all their artwork and awards. We did this by buying a 4'x8' sheet of sound board and a huge piece of remnant fabric. We covered the board with the fabric, and Dalton helped us hang everything on it. We actually have

- two of these hanging in the hallway where we see them multiple times a day.
- ♥ Making collages of their pictures all over your home and then playing "I spy..." We did this by setting up the scene of the picture and then whoever found the picture first won a prize.
- ♥ Birthday parties every year to celebrate their birth. Spend the morning making birthday cake together and the rest of the day celebrating them by doing things they want to do.

Song: Celebrate
Written and Performed by Kool & the Gang

Dalton's last Whataburger and vanilla malt with John in Phoenix, AZ - 12/24/2013

18

Time to Eat

Whether eating at home or eating elsewhere, at ANY age, it is a time for individual and/or family growth. It is NOT a place for toys, phones, electronics, or work. It's a great time to talk to each other and to learn about what's going on in everyone's life: new friends and old ones, schedules, daily activities, stresses or worries, school projects, work projects, etc. It's also a great time to discuss life lessons (like using manners, "please" and "thank you," what to do when you're eating alone, etc.). There really is a lot to talk about during every single meal of the day. And, if you or your child are eating alone, it's also a great time to plan the day or week or think about things that are good, bad, happy, or sad.

I cannot begin to tell you the number of times we have been out to dinner and seen another family staring at their phones rather than talking to each other. It's maddening to think that everyone, *especially the parents*, is on their phones setting the example for their children that this is an acceptable behavior, rather than using that time to their advantage to communicate with their children! For a parent who would do ANYTHING to have one single minute of that time with their child *just one more time* (one more breakfast, one more lunch, one more dinner, one more Molten Chocolate Cake at Chili's), it is *extremely* stressful to watch it in action. It usually takes my husband literally holding me back for me not to smack them into reality. What we have started doing is buying dessert for those families and sending them a written message with two Pay It Forward Cards in Dalton's memory (you'll learn more about these cards in the *Pay It Forward* chapter). Hopefully, that's a bit more effective than me going bonkers in a restaurant.

Our last dinner with Dalton was spent around a campfire eating steak. We were camping with friends, and as we sat in our camp chairs eating, we went around the circle saying what we were thankful for. Just after that meal, after everyone else had gotten up to take care of their plates, I asked Dalton if he was doing okay. Laying sideways in his camp chair, staring up in the sky, with his greenish-blue hoodie nearly covering his face, he looked up at me and said, "I'm totally content with my life right now." I was flabbergasted. What 15-year-old says that?!?! It was a really beautiful moment when all felt right with the world; like we had really done this parenting thing right. Had I been on my phone, or distracted by something else, I would have missed that entire unplanned, beautiful moment. So please, *I beg you...* put everything away except the food and drink and focus on your children at mealtimes. You never know. They could be gone forever less than 15 hours later.

Straightforward Tips for Parenting at Your Best

Have a regimen when eating at home where toys and electronics (including phones) do not come near the dinner table *for any reason*. Make this a fun time. Ask questions about their day, their friends, their activities, what they learned today that they didn't know yesterday, etc. Also, be sure

> Had I been on my phone, or distracted by something else, I would have missed that entire unplanned, beautiful moment.

to teach them to ask about you too. We live in a society where everyone is *all about themselves* and they always want to tell you *their story*, but seldom take the opportunity to hear about yours. Use this time as a teaching tool, teaching them when someone asks them something to respond properly, and then ask about the other person. (Example: *"I'm going to ask you a question about your day, and once I've listened to you tell me about your day, please ask me a question about my day."*) This will serve them well now and in the future. Better yet, it will help to create caring people in our society, and we need more of them!

> Use this time as a teaching tool, teaching them when someone asks them something to respond properly, and then ask about the other person.

Create a fun bag for eating out that will help curb the time waiting in a restaurant for your food to be served. The bag can include fun activities like coloring books and crayons, shapes, books, Legos®, flash cards, playing cards for games like Concentration, Slap Jack, Speed, Scrabble®, Uno®, Skipbo®, or any other fun card games you can find. When they are very young, shape cubes, step rings, and letter blocks are also great toys.

Cheerios® can also be fun to build with. Whatever it is, make sure it includes something that helps you focus as much attention on having fun with each other as it does on playing the game. Also, remember to teach them that when their food arrives, it's time to put the games away and focus on eating and communicating with each other. For your child, it keeps their brain busy and their butt in the seat, so that they're not disturbing other patrons or driving the waitstaff crazy. Additionally, it teaches them how to occupy themselves and others. Dalton was quite proud to share the games with his cousins and friends when we took them out to eat, too.

Teach your children at a young age how to order their own food politely by looking directly at the waitstaff and speaking loudly enough for them to hear, using their manners such as "please" and "thank you."

Another fun idea is to Google "dinner table discussion." There are tons of cool conversation starters out there! I also have some on my website www.ParentingAtYourBestWithoutRegrets.com.

As a side note, I challenge all restaurant owners to put phone baskets and explanation cards on each table for families to put their phones in while they are dining so that they are able to focus on each other during their meals, instead of their phones.

Song: Cheeseburger in Paradise
Written and Performed by Jimmy Buffett

Our first shot at taking family selfies, and our very last family picture.
Glamis, CA - 12/25/2013

19

Picture Perfect

If you're anything like me, you're the one always in control and always on the *backside* of the camera. That said, please be sure you take the opportunity to get in front of the camera with your children as often as you can. Take pictures and videos of the hugs and kisses, the funny times, laughter, friends, and celebrations.

There will be several times in your life when you need photos or videos of your child or family. Often times, teachers ask for them to make your child *Student of the Week* at school, or for a school project. You'll also want them organized for graduations, weddings, life celebrations, and other big events.

Straightforward Tips for Parenting at Your Best

Be IN the photos!

For special events, maybe ask another family member or friend to use your camera to take photos and videos, or hire someone with their own camera or a photo booth. That way, you can enjoy the moment, and also be in the photos with your child.

Always have your camera handy, but don't ever let it take precedence over enjoying the moment with your loved ones.

Plan a few hours each month to upload and organize your pictures by YEAR-MONTH-DAY-EVENT. I cannot stress this enough. We learned that "date taken" is often incorrect and, a lot of times, it isn't even there (especially on older photos). Organizing them this way allows you to see how time changes you and your loved ones. Additionally, it helps you know when you were at certain events in your lives.

Please back up everything on your cameras, phones, and computers daily. If you think you're already set up for this to automatically happen, TEST IT! We lost over 460 pictures from my phone that were scheduled to be backed up nightly and, in fact, the phone said they were backed up. I just trusted it and never checked. They weren't being backed up, and those photos of Dalton are gone forever.

Last, but certainly not least, always have your camera handy, but don't ever let it take precedence over enjoying the moment with your loved ones.

> Song: In Color
> Written by Jamey Johnson,
> Lee Thomas Miller, and James Otto
> Performed by Jamey Johnson

Dalton on Christmas Morning 2010 with his Ibanez guitar.

Music to My Ears

When I first found out I was pregnant, countless people told me that I had to listen to Mozart and Beethoven and other classical musicians to make my baby smarter and more compassionate. So, of course, I purchased their music and also added some of my own; mostly country music, some pop and rock, anything that would make the baby move inside my tummy. I used headphones and a Walkman Cassette Player (if you can remember what those were) and I played music with headphones on my stomach every chance I could. Typically, I had music playing in the house and the car and spoke and sang and danced a lot while the baby was growing inside me. It's said that a mother's voice and movement is music to an embryo's developing ears.

While we'll never know for a fact if doing so really did make Dalton smarter or more compassionate, I can tell you that he *did* recognize that particular music a few years later. I know this because, after Dalton was born, I put the Beethoven and Mozart music in a box at the top of his closet, and only found it years later when we were moving. When I played it, Dalton said he knew this music, and I'd never played it for him outside of my womb until that moment. (Just for the record, he *was* really smart, and he loved music and dancing.)

> Music became a great conversation starter and a safe way for us to speak to each other when words didn't come so easy.

Music has also spurred many conversations over the years, the first of which, when Dalton was really little, was about Phil Collin's *You'll Be In My Heart*, from the Tarzan movie. He asked me why I sang that song to him every night, and I explained that he would always be in my heart, no matter what, just like Tarzan was to Kala in the movie. The next questions came when Dalton was 4 or 5 years old, and we were listening to Dolly Parton's *Coat of Many Colors*. He asked me to play it again and again in the car, and then asked me to tell him what it meant, so I told him the story using the lyrics without the music and asked him what he thought it meant. Shortly after that conversation, he told me, "You know mom, you could make me a blanket from your old jammies, and that could be like *my* coat of many colors." I'm no seamstress, but all those old pajamas I had worn nearly to shreds became a huge, colorful blanket that he wrapped himself up in like a burrito every single night to go to sleep. It's a blanket we still use every night.

Dalton's "blanket of many colors" and the Artful Ashes Heart made from his cremains.

Those conversations evolved over the years to questions about lyrics in the music he and his friends listened to. It gave us the opportunity to discuss some tough subjects like suicide, teen pregnancy, bullying, falling in love, his first kiss, why music is so important in movies and relationships, when the right time is to have sex with someone you love, etc.

Music became a great conversation starter and a safe way for us to speak to each other when words didn't come so easy. It was always playing in the background at home and while we were driving or camping. Music is within nearly all of our memories; good and bad. It has also been very impactful in our grief journey.

Straightforward Tips for Parenting at Your Best

Not all families view music as a staple in their lives. As important as food is for the body, I believe music is for the soul.

You can use music as a tool for communicating with and educating your children, as well as for fun during long drives. You may find that the ABC's are easier to learn singing the alphabet song and that memorizing state capitols is easier if you can make up a song to help remember them. Additionally, upbeat music can often increase spirits and get everyone moving (which is something we need a lot more of in this world of electronics and laziness). Music can also be used to know how your child is feeling. If they are playing a sad song over and over, maybe your child needs someone to talk to. There are also some songs out there that tell the world to leave us alone. Maybe we're "helicopter parenting" or "lawn-mower parenting" and we need to give them some space. Obviously, every situation is different, but I could not imagine my life, *not even a day*, without music.

> Song: I Learned It On The Radio
> Written by Nicolle Galyon, Ashley Gorley, and Jimmy Robbins
> Performed by Thomas Rhett

Dalton dancing in the rain at Universal Studios in Orlando, Florida - 10/2007

Dance, Dance, Dance

My husband and I love to country dance (two-step, waltz, cha-cha, etc.), and we've gotten pretty good at it in over 21 years of marriage. We did our best to teach Dalton how to dance too. While he learned how to two-step and waltz, he really loved to just jam out to dubstep or eighties music. We danced a lot together around the house, usually while we were making dinner or cleaning. It was the one time that we were all completely free of self-consciousness. We weren't afraid to look funny, and the entire point was to laugh and enjoy ourselves. I've always found when dancing with John or with Dalton, there was nothing else in the world that mattered, and that's a great feeling.

Straightforward Tips for Parenting at Your Best

Dancing together is another way to show love and build confidence. Make it fun. Make it spur of the moment. Be crazy. Most of all, forget about what anybody else thinks of you.

Song: Like There's No Yesterday
Written by Chris Lindsey, Aimee Mayo, Troy Verges, and Brett James
Performed by Mark Wills

Dalton and his cousin, Mathew, just before the 52-Card-Pick-Up meltdown - 2/26/2005

Family Game Night

Few activities are better than spending a night playing games with family. When I go back in my memories as a child, I remember countless nights with my grandparents and all my aunts, uncles, and cousins at a huge dining room table, playing games, laughing uncontrollably, and having a blast. In the years since we've been married and had Dalton, I have even more memories of playing Catch Phrase®, Pictionary®, Scrabble®, Uno®, Dominoes, Hand-and-Foot, Speed, Apples to Apples®, Sequence®, Golf, Dice, Nasty, and even Cards Against Humanity®. All of these have been filled with laughter and excited anticipation of the next funny comment or action. And then there's Poker Night with all the neighbors, where we laugh so much, our stomachs and cheeks hurt for two days after it's over!

Not only is having a game night great entertainment, but it's also what I call "controlled sportsmanship training," especially when someone asks you to play 52-Card Pick-Up, and you're an exhausted 6-year-old who hasn't had a nap all day. That can quickly turn into a full-blown temper tantrum, but it can also turn into a great teaching moment.

> Few activities are better than spending a night playing games with family.

Straightforward Tips for Parenting at Your Best

- ♥ Schedule game nights with family and friends on a monthly basis (or more, if possible).
- ♥ Find games that are age-appropriate for your family and fun for everyone.
- ♥ For gifts, give games. (I'm a huge proponent of giving games as wedding gifts too because *the family that plays together, stays together!*)
- ♥ Expect some time-outs with young children and grumpy grandpas, but all-in-all, enjoy your time together.

Song: Smile
Written by Uncle Kracker, Blair Daly,
J.T. Harding, and Jeremy Bose
Performed by Uncle Kracker

Mommy says: "Hey Deej. Do you remember what that building is?"

Dalton says: "Yeah, Mommy. That's where you got married!"

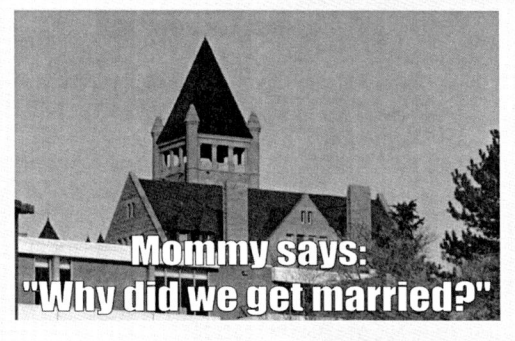

Mommy says: "Why did we get married?"

Dalton says: "So you could have me, mommy!!!"

23

Words and Events That Alter Your Vocabulary

As a family, the first one of these words for us was *"calapitter,"* because Dalton could not figure out how to say, "caterpillar." To this day, every time John and I are in conversation about something that involves the topic of caterpillars, we always slip and say *"calapitter."*

For Dalton's first 19 months of life, he had chronic ear infections, which he later referred to as *"ear conflexions,"* and so we also use that term when discussing ear infections now.

We've found this is fun to do with music as well. There are so many songs out there where we mistake the lyrics for something else. In Kenny Rogers song, *"Lucille,"* the lyric is, "Four *hungry* children and a crop in the field." I could never understand how the guy in the song had "four-*hundred* children." One day, I asked John if that's really what the song said and he and Dalton laughed and laughed and laughed. Apparently, I'm quite funny. So now, every time we hear that song, we sing at the top of our lungs, "four-*hundred* children and a crop in the field!" While it may sound cheesy, it's just another funny memory that I am glad we have.

> *Make it worth your children's time and energy to learn about words and grammar and how to play-on-words.*

Another version of this is in terms that are generated after tragic events occur, such as "9/11," "Columbine," or "Orlando." The second you use one of these terms, people know *exactly* what you're referring to. There will most certainly be these types of terms created in your children's lifetimes too. Keep track of them. For our family, we now have "before" and "after" Dalton went to Heaven as words that have altered our vocabulary as well.

Straightforward Tips for Parenting at Your Best

While it's important to correct our children when they use the wrong vocabulary, it's also good to make it fun when we're correcting them. When these moments happen, write the words they used and also their real meanings in your child's journal (you know, the one you're writing because I told you about it several chapters ago?). Also, keep track of those words or phrases that are new during their lifetime. For me, words like "cell phone," "texting," "Twitter," and "Facebook," are all new since I was born.

Also, work on vocabulary and enunciation by listening to fun, fast-paced songs. Some that we had fun using with Dalton were:

- ♥ Charlie Daniels Band – The Devil Went Down To Georgia
- ♥ John Michael Montgomery – Be My Baby Tonight
- ♥ John Michael Montgomery - Sold
- ♥ Josh Gracin – Nothin' To Lose
- ♥ Rodney Atkins - If You're Going Through Hell
- ♥ The Tractors - Baby Likes to Rock It
- ♥ Toby Keith – Who's Your Daddy
- ♥ Trace Adkins - Honkytonk Badonkadonk
- ♥ Travis Tritt - T-r-o-u-b-l-e

Have fun with words. Play with them. Teach your children how they can be turned around to be happy, sad, funny, or hurtful. Make it worth your children's time and energy to learn about words and grammar and how to *play-on-words*. Country singers, Brad Paisley and Eric Church, are masters at manipulating lyrics for multiple meanings/innuendos in their music. Go find some that make you giggle.

> Song: Anything Like Me
> Written by: Charles Dubois, Brad Paisley, and Dave Turnbull
> Performed by Brad Paisley

Dalton and Sam on our trip to Texas - Spring Break 2013

On our way home from Glamis after Dalton's 1st Anniversary in Heaven.

Road Trip!

From the time I was a little girl, road trips were always my favorite activity. It meant I had my family all to myself, and it meant we would sing! We drove a lot of miles back and forth to many places spending 6-8 hours in the car at a time. We continued that tradition with Dalton, always driving, rather than flying, whenever it was possible, often taking Dalton's friends or cousins along.

Straightforward Tips for Parenting at Your Best

- ♥ Prepare your music ahead of time. Using an iPod helps a lot with this, making sure that everyone's musical tastes are included. Plan how the musical time is spent and agree that there's no complaining about anyone else's music.
- ♥ Have plenty of snacks and drinks on hand.
- ♥ Take a sealed baggie with a few wet washcloths inside for cleaning dirty faces and hands.
- ♥ Take a roll of paper towels just in case there are any spills.
- ♥ Remember your travel journals (discussed in Chapter 1).
- ♥ Plan games for the ride. There are quite a few books and websites available that have great ideas for road trip games.
- ♥ Take a real map that you actually open and look at. Use this as a teaching tool when you stop along the way to see where you've been and where you're going. Draw your route on the map with a marker.
- ♥ Even though excitement will usually rush you, plan your trips so that you're not rushed to get out of town, and leave an extra day at the tail end just in case you have car troubles (spoken from lots of experience).
- ♥ Leave before or after rush-hour traffic. Nothing

ruins a road trip faster than being excited to get on the open road and being stuck behind 25,000 bumper-to-bumper drivers.
- ♥ We used to plan exactly where we'd stop, booking motels or finding places to park the camper before we ever left the house, but we've found that being spontaneous is often more fun. For some people, being spontaneous is way out of their comfort zone and may cause a lot of anxiety. For others, planning may cause more anxiety than what it's worth. Do what makes you comfortable.
- ♥ Enjoy your time together and take lots of photos and videos!

Song: Convoy
Written by C.W. McCall and Chip Davis
Performed by C.W. McCall

Kelly Brown paying tribute to his "Shadow."
Photo by Andrew Hiniker.

Events That Transform Our Lives

As John and I move deeper and deeper into our grief journey, it's become quite obvious to me that our everyday world does *not* teach people about grief - how to handle it, how to help others during their grief journey, or even simple things (you would think), like what *not* to say.

Thankfully, not everyone will have to endure tragedy in their lives. Still, it's important to know how to react when someone else is struggling so that your words and actions *help* rather than *hinder*.

You may wonder why I bring this up in a book about parenting. I believe it's extremely important to begin teaching our children about grief, compassion, and helping others at a young age so they are better at it as they go through school and become adults. Hopefully, it will then be passed down to future generations.

It's important to realize that words are often spoken out of context because most people don't have any idea what to say. Nothing you or I say will bring someone back from the dead, from a terrible accident or disease, or from divorce or job loss. What your words *do* convey, though, is your willingness to *be present*; to *listen*, to *love*, to *support*. Most times, just saying their loved one's name or saying *nothing at all* is the best option.

> It's important to know how to react when someone else is struggling so that your words and actions help rather than hinder.

There's a great blog written about the words people say after someone they know has faced tragedy. It's written by a wonderful woman whose words are so eloquently written in everything she writes, and she is a bright light in what seems like a pretty dark world for those of us who have lost children. I hope to meet this woman someday.

Angela Miller is a writer, speaker, and grief advocate who provides support and solace to those who are grieving the loss of a child. She is the author of *You Are the Mother Of All Mothers: A Message Of Hope For the Grieving Heart,* founder of the award-winning online community *A Bed For My Heart* and writer for the Open to Hope Foundation and Still Standing Magazine. All of her posts really speak to me, but this one fit so well in this chapter...

Easy For You To Say
written March 27, 2013, by Angela Miller

A couple months ago, after having one too many clichés flung in my face, through a mess of tears, I wrote this. Then I daydreamed about the next time someone clichés all over me- instead of nodding and smiling while crying inside, or kindly educating them about a more comforting and helpful way to talk to a bereaved parent- I'd have enough grit and grace to recite this instead:

Easy for you to say God needed another angel—
since God didn't ask you for yours.
Easy for you to say God has a plan—

*if all of God's plans for you have precisely tailgated your own like
a lovely fairy tale.
Easy for you to say everything happens for a reason—
please tell me one good reason my son
is forever buried deep underground?
Easy for you to say trust God—
if you've never felt betrayed by the heavens themselves.
Easy for you to say hang on to hope—
if you can still find your rope.
Easy for you to say time heals all wounds—
if time has already made perfect
heart-shaped scabs of yours.
Easy for you to say be thankful for what you have—
would you like to switch places with me
and feel how little I have left?
Easy for you to say God needed
another flower for his garden—
if none of your 'flowers' have ever
been plucked before their time.
Easy for you to say find peace and move on—
if you haven't had to hold your dead child's hand
inside the curves of your living one.
Easy for you to say he's in a better place—
if you still get to hold your child in the best place there is.
Easy for you to say you're young, you can have more—
would you be willing to exchange your living child for those you*

might someday have?
Easy for you to say every cloud has a silver lining—
if you haven't been asked to walk through this never-ending storm of mine.
Easy for you to say it was God's will—
if the plan you got currently includes all of your children rambunctiously romping around your living room.

―※―

I shared this on my Facebook page, and the comments were wonderful. People shared their fear of never knowing what to say, admitted to saying so many of these phrases, and most importantly, learned from what both Angela and I, and so many others, have to face every day for the rest of our lives - waking up *without* our children. If there's *anything* in my grief journey I wish to do, it is to share with others anything I can to make this world a brighter place to live in.

Straightforward Tips for Parenting at Your Best

As a supporter of someone grieving, there are many wonderful things we can do to help each other. I'll start with the list of things I have learned were helpful for us after Dalton left for Heaven...

- ♥ Be sure to talk about their loved one every chance you get. Say their name! Make them important. They DID exist. They were here, and their life mattered. It still matters.
- ♥ Talk about their loved one and write down any memories you have of them in vivid detail.
- ♥ Help them make notes of everything, because what they are going through will not allow them to process or remember much for a very long time.

> Help them count their blessings.

- ♥ Sit down with them and write or record what happened the days and weeks previous to the death(s), starting with today and moving backward.
- ♥ Go through their photos by hand and/or on the computer and sort them Year-Month-Date-Event as this will help them sort for the life celebration/funeral, as well as for looking at/watching in order later. It also helps stir up the good memories, and they need to be reminded of those every chance you get.
- ♥ If they are cremating their loved one, there's no need to have a service right away. People who are

grieving can take time and plan something creative that would mean something more to everyone later, rather than just being a blur of people they can't remember when it's over.
- ♥ If they are doing a service, lighten it up by having family and friends speak and tell funny stories about the deceased. Be sure to video this so they can watch it in a few years when the numb wears off.
- ♥ Create a spreadsheet to track names, addresses, phone numbers, emails, gifts, cards, donations, etc. Later, they can write thank you cards and remember who did/sent what (you wouldn't believe how many people ask how the plant they sent is growing, or what was done with the money they sent). At Dalton's service, I actually had five friends bring their laptops and, in lieu of a guestbook, people checked in on the Excel spreadsheet. This was so helpful!
- ♥ If the loved one who passed away was a Facebook or other social media user, it would be good to gather screenshots of each of their posts before they passed, as well as those condolences that will come through on social media, and put them into a binder.
- ♥ Make sure they have water, toiletries, and paper

goods at their house. It's crazy the amount of toilet paper that is used!
- ♥ Keurig coffee makers are very helpful (We were making full pots of coffee for one or two visitors at a time and then dumping them out, so one cup at a time was very helpful).
- ♥ KEEP THEM BUSY! I cannot stress this enough. Assist them in going through pictures and belongings, listen to their memories pour out (no need to speak; just listen), watch movies, play games, keep their mind and body active. Get them back to work ASAP. Laying around makes the pain so much worse!!!!
- ♥ Help them find a way to help others. It takes the focus off their own loss and focuses their energy on someone else in need.
- ♥ As far as gifts go, gift cards for food and movies are great as they get them out of the house and remind them to eat.
- ♥ If they are open to it, finding a counselor or a grief support group may be helpful. GriefShare and Compassionate Friends were the ones most recommended to us.
- ♥ Encourage them to be blatantly honest when people ask questions about the death, as it helps curb questions later. And, when it's a child who

has passed, being open to questions from that child's friends is *very* important, as knowing the "who," "what," and "how" seems to help younger minds along in their grief journey.
- ♥ If you hear beautiful music or see a video or movie or story that reminds you of their loved one, please share it with them. It's nice to know their loved one is remembered.
- ♥ Help them count their blessings.
- ♥ Help them make a very deliberate decision to be thankful that people are trying to help, even when they say/do the wrong things. That said, let others know that it is perfectly okay NOT to know what to say, as NOTHING anyone can say will bring their loved one back. I'd rather you say, "I don't know what to say," than to use a cliché about *God needing another angel.* When people *do* say hurtful things (and *they will*), remind the griever to bite their tongue, remembering to be thankful that people care enough to even *try* to say something.
- ♥ Have them keep in touch with friends of their loved one. Stay involved with the friends, as it's neat to watch how they'll grow and change. That way, they can get a glimpse of what their angel might be like if they were here today.

♥ Set reminders in your calendar to call or send a card four months out and every few months after that, as it seems like everyone forgets at the 4-month-mark.
♥ Additionally, it was very helpful for us to do a "Grief Letter," which was a letter explaining how we were doing, what we had been doing to keep busy, thank you's, etc. It helps curb the questions from people that they'll be answering so often. It also helps people to see where they are at, literally and figuratively. We did one a few months after Dalton passed and also again at the 1st and 2nd anniversary. This idea came from the Compassionate Friends meeting I attended. It was helpful for our family and friends to learn about where we were in our journey, and it was also very healing for me to write it. Our letters can be viewed at www.DoItForDalton.com to give them an idea of where to begin.
♥ Great options for memorial gifts can be found at www.PerfectMemorials.com and www.ArtfulAshes.com.

And, last, but not least, everyone has their own religious/spiritual beliefs. We have been very open to listening to what people have to say. We take what we like, discard the rest, and have made up our own little belief system. We count our blessings every day that we had those precious years with Dalton and are very thankful for the countless memories we all made together in that short period of time.

Death is not a matter of "if," it is a matter of "when," therefore we should all be taught how to help those going through the loss of a loved one.

> Song: If Everyone Cared
> Written by Chad Kroeger, Michael Kroeger, Ryan Peake, Ryan Anthony, and Daniel Adair
> Performed by Nickelback

Our last photo of Dalton (with Brennan, our godson)
Glamis, CA - 12/28/2013

Advance Arrangements

Have you ever heard comments like:

- "Before he died, he told me everything was in the bottom drawer of his desk, but I can't find it anywhere now!"
- "The ER nurse is asking for a list of my mom's medications and the doctor's office isn't open until the morning to give me that information."
- "My purse was stolen and, while I was trying to locate phone numbers to call all my credit card companies to cancel the cards, the thieves were buying electronics on the internet."
- "I'm trying to refinance my house, and you'd think the

bank needed my first born kid with all the information they asked for! I spent hours trying to locate everything."

Back in 2011, my mom and I had an idea to begin a company, *Advance Arrangements*, to help people take control of these issues using a website designed to put everything in *one location* so everyone and their trusted loved ones would have just *one* place to go for everything needed in a time of crisis. The idea was that a person completed the information and updated it *as life changed*, so if the unforeseen happened, everyone designated would be "in-the-know."

> *Professionals call this Estate Planning. I call it taking care of your family.*

We believed in this idea so strongly that we spent much of our retirement savings to make it come alive, hoping that someday Google or Facebook or some other large investor would catch on and buy the idea making it a worldwide database to help families. No such luck. (*Just in case they are reading this, though, we still have all the info to make it go again.*)

While our idea didn't work for the masses, it made a huge difference in our own lives for the four years we had it, and I am still a HUGE proponent of making sure everyone has a plan for their loved ones upon their death or incapacitation. Professionals call this *Estate Planning*. I call it *taking care of your family*. This should be a law - our military is required to put their plans in writing - why aren't we, the general public?

After losing Dalton, it's now real to us that life can end at any second, and we MUST be sure our families are aware of our plans. This goes all the way from how we want to be laid to rest, to songs we want to have played at our services, to making sure there is life insurance to fund the services and living expenses while our loved ones get back on their feet, etc. Leaving this undone is a crime, as it's just another layer of grief to those left behind.

This is a blog I wrote quite a while ago, and it still holds true...

The Time to Buy Life Insurance is Now

As most of you know, I lost my only child in an ATV accident over Christmas break. Dalton was only 15 years old, and our entire world revolved around him. The grief that goes along with losing a child is unimaginable and beyond explanation. It's baffling what emotions can do to your brain and how they affect your every move and decision, if you can even make decisions. I have a hard time even figuring out how to move one foot in front of the other these days. That said, I am so very thankful for my brain working in 2012 when I finally purchased life insurance for my son and each of my sister's children.

I never intended to actually use the life insurance for its purpose, as the inexpensive policies I purchased carried a guarantee that would help each of the kids later in life, where they could raise the death benefit up to $450k, without ever having to re-qualify for the insurance. To me, that was a safety worth paying for, just in case any of them ended up with a debilitating disease that would not allow them to qualify for life insurance later in life.

Dalton's accident happened in California, so we had to cover all of the standard expenses there, as well as covering them again, here in Colorado. Then, there was the added cost of transporting him home in the proper container at the proper temperature, paying the funeral home in California to work with the funeral home here, then paying for the casket here for the viewing (because the box we brought him home in was not for viewing). Then we had the blessing, celebration of life, programs, pictures, urns, cremation, food and drinks to feed everyone while they were here, travel expenses, etc. With all the expenses, this could have bankrupted us. As of today, we have incurred over $21,000, not including any of the time we've spent away from work, or medical expenses *incurred at the accident scene.*

Had I not spent the $60/year for the life insurance policy I bought for Dalton, we never would have been able to give him the celebration his short, beautiful life deserved, nor could we have made our house payment, or paid any other bills from then until now. More importantly, though, we would not have had the brainpower to figure out how to make it all work. That, in itself, proves to me that life insurance is something which must be budgeted for every single month.

So, please, if you have children, grandchildren, nieces, nephews, or friends with children, who do not have life insurance, there are so many other benefits more than just a death benefit. Please, look into it for a birthday or Christmas gift or just because. It's worth it just for the guarantee that they'll be covered when they grow up and have babies of their own.

My husband and I never dreamed this could happen to our son, but it did. Please think about it, and then DO something about it. Waiting until tomorrow could be too late.

Straightforward Tips for Parenting at Your Best

♥ While our *Advance Arrangements* website is no longer active, there is a workbook you can purchase

PARENTING AT YOUR BEST

which is quite helpful to get things in order at http://Organize-You.com/. The creator, Mary Kelly, Ph.D., is someone I met in 2013, and her workbook has much of the same information as our website did. I fully endorse Mary's workbook as a great starting point for everyone. As Mary says, "If you are old enough to have a driver's license, you need to be organized."

- ♥ Referrals are always the best ways to find good people to help you with estate planning. Ask your trusted friends and family who they use for life insurance and estate planning.
- ♥ Call and set up a time to meet both an attorney and a financial planner. Time is of the essence!
- ♥ Figure out a way to fit life insurance into your budget. It could mean the difference of your family eating or starving when you're gone!

Song: Don't Blink
Written by Chris Allen Wallin and Casey Michael Beathard
Performed by Kenny Chesney

The beautiful homecoming tribute, much like the end of the Pay It Forward movie, from our amazing Beverly Hillbillies, family, and friends, all put together by Dalton's close friend and neighbor, Alexis - January 5, 2014

27

Pay It Forward

Have you ever heard the song, *Chain of Love*, by Clay Walker? If not, it's well worth a listen once, or a hundred times. That song and the book-turned-movie *Pay It Forward*, written by Catherine Ryan Hyde and Leslie Dixon, are both extremely well written.

While we lived our lives this way long before we heard or saw the song, the book, and the movie, all three have been great reminders that daily acts of kindness can change the world. Maybe not the *whole* world, but someone's small place in this big world can *always* be affected by a random act of kindness.

As the song goes, a woman gets a flat tire, and a man

changes it for her. He refuses any payment from her, so when she stops to eat a few miles down the road, she decides to give a tired, pregnant waitress a large tip. The waitress takes that money home to share with her husband, who just happens to be the same guy who changed the woman's tire in the first place. Thus, kindness came full circle.

The movie, on the other hand, has a teenager figuring out a project that can change the world by performing a random act of kindness for three different people and then asking those three people to *Pay It Forward* to keep the chain going, and so on. The movie shows how one boys' three small acts of kindness spread all over the nation like wildfire. While you may think it's a little far-fetched, when Dalton passed away, we started our own *Pay It Forward* campaign and the little cards we made in Dalton's memory have spread to many states in the U.S., as well as to several other countries. It's been very telling for us that our son's life, and the impact he made, was not just that of a 15-year-old kid, but one of a legacy that will go on for many years.

> Someone's small place in this big world can always be affected by a random act of kindness.

These are the Pay It Forward cards we had made to give out when we practice random acts of kindness for others.

In Loving Memory of Dalton Lambrecht
4/25/1998-12/29/2013 - Age 15

Dalton lived his short life with the intent to create smiles, laughter, and happiness by sharing his kind spirit and helping others through tough times.

Compliments of:_____

May you take this simple act of kindness and Pay It Forward in Dalton's name to keep his legacy traveling around the world and then share it with us on his website at

www.DoItForDalton.com

Something else we had discussed as a family was organ donation and Dalton was all for it. When he passed away, we were in Glamis, CA, far from a hospital, and his organs could not be harvested fast enough to be donated. He had the most beautiful heart and the deepest brown eyes. He was so healthy. I wish we could have helped someone else with his organs, but that was not in the greater plan, a fact that has been *very* frustrating for us. A short time ago, though, one of my friends lost her brother, and she recently found out that his eyes had helped someone see again. The joy it brought her to know that her brother's life had made a difference in someone else's life was beautiful to witness.

Straightforward Tips for Parenting at Your Best

While organ donation is the largest form of paying it forward, small acts of kindness are beautiful too. If everyone did just ONE nice thing for someone else each and every day, just think of the world we could live in!

> If everyone did just ONE nice thing for someone else each and every day, just think of the world we could live in!

I challenge you and your family to find a person or family in need and make a conscious effort to help them. Make meals to help them through a tough time, help them get their next big break by using your sphere of influence, read to them, mow their yard, clean their house, or wash their car. You could pay their electric bill, get them out of the house for a walk, a movie, a meal, or just have a conversation. Give your next waiter or waitress a tip they will be happily surprised to receive, or just smile at the next stranger you see. PLEASE DO IT! Get your family involved. And then, if/when it's appropriate, ask that person to *Pay It Forward* to someone else in need.

I also ask you to visit www.DonateLife.net and register to be an organ, eye, and tissue donor. You can also do this at your local motor vehicle office.

> *"At the end of the day, it's not about what you have,*
> *or even what you've accomplished.*
> *It's about what you've done with those accomplishments.*
> *It's about who you've lifted up, who you've made better.*
> *It's about what you've given back."*
> -Denzel Washington,
> from his book, *A Hand to Guide Me*

Song: Chain of Love
Written by Clay Walker and Rory Feek
Performed by Clay Walker

The love of cousins...
Mathew, Dalton, and Steven celebrating Dalton's 1st Birthday - 4/30/1999

Neighbors and best friends forever...
Dominic, Dalton, and Alexis - May 2004

Feed The People Who Feed You

One of the first lessons I learned in business is that a lot of people are takers. They take your time, take your product samples, let you take them to lunch, and take advantage of you however they can. I quickly decided I was not going to be one of those people, as it's always much more rewarding to know you've worked with and/or helped someone who appreciates it.

I've built my business relationships by being the first in the feeding chain, meaning when I needed my windshield repaired, I heard my neighbor did that for a living, so I called him. He did a great job for a reasonable price so I added him to the list of people whom I feel comfortable referring to others. In turn, he has told friends and family about my business, and we now have a trusting, reciprocal relationship. We are happy to refer each other to friends and family. This is not rocket science. Every successful business person builds their own "sphere of influence," yet you'd be surprised how many of those successful business people don't realize that the same premise works in their personal lives with family, friends, and neighbors.

We always did our best to teach Dalton that if he wanted a friend, he would need to introduce himself and begin a conversation. If that person responded kindly and they found a rhythm in their conversation that was comfortable, maybe that person would end up becoming a friend. In most cases, Dalton was lucky enough to have amazing friends, but a few times, he learned lessons instead.

Feeding those that feed you in your personal life means that if someone builds you up with their words, makes you laugh, enjoys their time with you, and you do the same for them, you're "feeding" each other. On the other hand, if someone is constantly borrowing your notes, borrowing your lunch money, making commitments they don't keep, saying mean things about you, all-in-all taking the food *off* your plate and never replenishing it, then you need to show that someone the exit door. This includes family too. Enabling others to take advantage of you is an accident *once*. If you give them the opportunity to do it again, you only have yourself to blame.

Straightforward Tips for Parenting at Your Best

By our own example, we always taught Dalton to surround himself with wonderful people and he learned that lesson very well. We were always very vocal about the people we had in our lives, and Dalton was usually involved in those conversations. If there was some sort of struggle going on, we would all take the time to discuss what we "brought" to this person, be it friendship or moral support, or sharing their name with others who could bring them success. If they needed us, would we drop everything to be there? Then we would discuss what they "brought" to our lives. Are we happy when we are with them? Do they support us? Are they loyal to our friendship? If we needed them, would they be there? Do they represent a victim mentality that makes us sad to be around them? Do we want to continue to be around that? Having open conversations about relationships has always been very helpful for our family.

> *In our own lives and especially those of our children, we must pay attention and be aware of whom we are surrounding ourselves with and how our own actions and words may affect others.*

In our own lives and especially those of our children, we must pay attention and be aware of whom we are surrounding ourselves with and how our own actions and words may affect others. We must also be mindful of our actions and conversations to and about our family, friends, and educators in front of our children.

Be involved with your child's friends and their parents. Know the who, what, when, where, why, and how *every single time* your child will be hosted by another family. Be sure to communicate the same information with other parents if you are hosting their child. Volunteer regularly in your child's classroom so you can get to know your child in their daily environment. Get to know their teachers, advisors, and other students. Bottom line: know who's feeding your child when you're not around and know what your child is dishing out.

> "As you grow older, you will discover that you have two hands; one for helping yourself, the other for helping others."
> -Audrey Hepburn

Song: Lean On Me
Written and Performed by Bill Withers

Funny selfie that Dalton posted in 2013
as he was learning to shave.

29

Common Sense Ain't So Common

People tell jokes on Facebook about being glad they grew up "back then," *before* their every move could be caught on social media for the entire world to see. I agree. I cannot imagine some of the dumb things I said or did ending up out there for my entire sphere to laugh at. I was bullied enough *without social media*. Nowadays, though, from a very young age, kids are faced with cell phones, texting, the internet, and social media.

While Dalton was alive, these were always topics of discussion, and I was a "freak" (according to Dalton) about user names and passwords and followed his every move via texts and social media. Yes, I monitored them *every day and night at unexpected times.*

In the hours, days, and months following Dalton's passing, social media was both a monster and a friend to us...

Scenario:

We were on vacation in California when Dalton passed away at 11:37AM MST. I didn't know until 1:59PM MST. Our friends, Kelly & Sonya, helped us make phone calls to family in Texas and South Dakota between 2PM and 4PM MST.

In Texas, one of Dalton's cousins knew a friend of Dalton's at home in Colorado. She called that friend, who did not yet know, and shared the news, not asking or realizing that Dalton's friend was alone and *not* in a situation of support to hear that kind of news. That friend, too sad to speak and not knowing what to do, texted another friend the news.

Someone's brilliant teenager ended up on Dalton's Facebook page and posted, "*Are you dead dude?*" I had Dalton's cell phone and had access to his Facebook account, but at that time, posts could not be deleted using cell phones, so I had no way of deleting the post. A real computer with internet would have been required, and we had no access to that in the middle of the California desert, nor did I know Dalton's Facebook password off the top of my head. It was at home. It took quite some time with my fuzzy brain to figure out how to reach the brilliant teenager to get the post off of Facebook. The stress those four little words caused us is beyond explanation.

This all had happened *four hours BEFORE* my family had even been notified. They were driving back to Colorado from South Dakota and, for their safety, we didn't want them to find out on the road. They were finally notified after 8PM MST.

I cannot imagine how much differently that scenario would have been had my family found out on Facebook while they were traveling, and I'm so glad we never had to learn.

On the flip side, we received countless beautiful messages from friends and strangers once they heard the news on Dalton's Facebook, my Facebook, as well as LinkedIn. Those messages were a huge support for us in the five days we spent waiting to bring Dalton home from California, during the 17-hour drive, and they still are today. Additionally, social media was the best location to share information for the celebration of life and scheduling activities with his friends. (We learned that most people don't even use the newspaper anymore to post these types of things because it is so cost prohibitive. The main newspaper in Colorado wanted over $700 to post Dalton's obituary. Shame on newspaper giants for being so greedy during a time of such intense suffering!)

Straightforward Tips for Parenting at Your Best

There should be some common sense rules when allowing your kids to use cell phones/texting/social media:

- ♥ Most important, require kids to share EVERY username and password for EVERY device, app, and website they have access to. Remind them *every night* to update you with new ones they created that day.
- ♥ Unkind or hurtful words/photos/videos are not allowed.
- ♥ Showing any skin is off-limits. Pictures/videos of people/selfies should be off-limits. Who really wants to see hundreds of selfies of ego-driven people anyway?
- ♥ If the story is not yours to share, STOP and keep your fingers off the buttons.
- ♥ Grief is not something to toy with, and it comes in

all areas of life; failing a test, losing a job, getting in trouble for something you or a friend did, break-ups, and death. It is NOT to be discussed over the phone, via text, or on the web. It is certainly not to be discussed outside your home until parents know what is going on and have had time to discuss it with their kids and have given their kids permission to discuss it outside of their home.

> *If you're going to be texting or using social media, do it to make the world a better place, not to add negativity.*

- ♥ Any bad news must only be shared if someone has a support system in place *and with them*, at the moment they are notified and after.
- ♥ When kids begin driving, require that phones and any other electronics are to be put away and out of reach anytime they are driving.
- ♥ Require that phone use ends at a certain time each evening and is not allowed at all during school hours, unless there's a legitimate emergency (example: Columbine).
- ♥ Phones should never be allowed during a meal by

anyone in the family.
- ♥ Remember social media is forever. As relationships change and comments are posted, consequences may arise later when you're looking for a job or building new relationships.
- ♥ Know when to step away from cell phones, texting, and social media.
- ♥ If you're going to be texting or using social media, do it to make the world a *better* place, not to add negativity.

> Song: Voices
> Written by Chris Young, Chris Tompkins, and Craig Wiseman
> Performed by Chris Young

In Loving Memory of Dalton John Lambrecht
4/25/1998-12/29/2013

30

Best Laid Plans

We would do nearly anything to help other parents avoid regret. In fact, the entire process for this book began when my husband asked if there was any way we could help other parents live without the regrets he endures every day now that Dalton is gone. While we know first-hand that this is easier said than done, we cannot play the blame game in any area of our lives, *especially when it comes to parenting.*

We speak with a lot of parents now. Many, like us, who have lost their children and others who are struggling as they watch their children make poor decisions, living lives of addiction, living with abusive partners, etc. As a general perception, when a child does well, parents don't usually give themselves any credit (they usually bestow that honor on their children), yet they tend to blame *themselves* for any bad place their child ends up, asking themselves what they did to lead their child to death or destructive behavior.

When a child is struggling or has left Earth too soon, one of the most poignant questions we can ask ourselves is this: "Is this what I dreamed for my child?" In every case, the answer is "No," because, as parents, we plan long, beautiful lives for our children, filled with smiles, laughter, confidence, independence, responsibility, self-awareness, and a heart full of love for others.

We *never* plan for them to die at a young age, to have a debilitating disease, to be an addict, or to become a teen parent. And we certainly never wish our child would believe suicide was their only option. When tough circumstances arise, it is very important to remember exactly what our original goals were and are for our child, as it will help remind us *not* to blame ourselves and help relieve us of our regrets (some of them, not all).

Straightforward Tips for Parenting at Your Best

Inevitably, our best-laid plans go awry. And while we cannot prepare for every situation or tragedy, we *can* choose the mindset in which we deal with it.

Write down your hopes and dreams for your child. Ask your child what their own hopes and dreams are. When they're old enough, have them write their dreams on a sheet of paper and save it. Do this often and save each one. Discuss the steps it will take to reach those dreams. As they get older, have this conversation with your child regularly, keeping in mind that hopes and dreams turn into goals, and they change over time, which means the paths to reach them will change too. Discuss in detail how they can attain their goals and at what lengths you are willing and able to help them.

> Failures now are far less expensive in every way than when they are over 18.

Allow them the freedom to fail while they are young. Failures now are far less expensive *in every way* than when they are over 18. Be clear about the lines between being a good parent and going overboard (now called a "lawnmower" parent), knowing that reaching a goal when you've done the majority of the work yourself, with a good support team behind you, means *far more* than having it handed to you.

Most important, though, take the time to make memories.

Special memories aren't always those big events or

costly outings. In fact, most of them are little everyday things, like cuddling, discussing highs and lows, making dinner, or doing laundry together. Cherish each one of them. Write them down. And always make sure your child knows they are the center of your world, because then, *no matter what happens*, you know you've done your job well, and it's hard to have regrets when you know you've done your best.

> Song: *You'll Always Be My Baby*
> Written by Sara Evans, Tom Shapiro, and Tony Martin
> Performed by Sara Evans
>
> and
>
> Song: *Send 'Em On Down The Road*
> Written by Marc Beeson and Allen Shamblin
> Performed by Garth Brooks

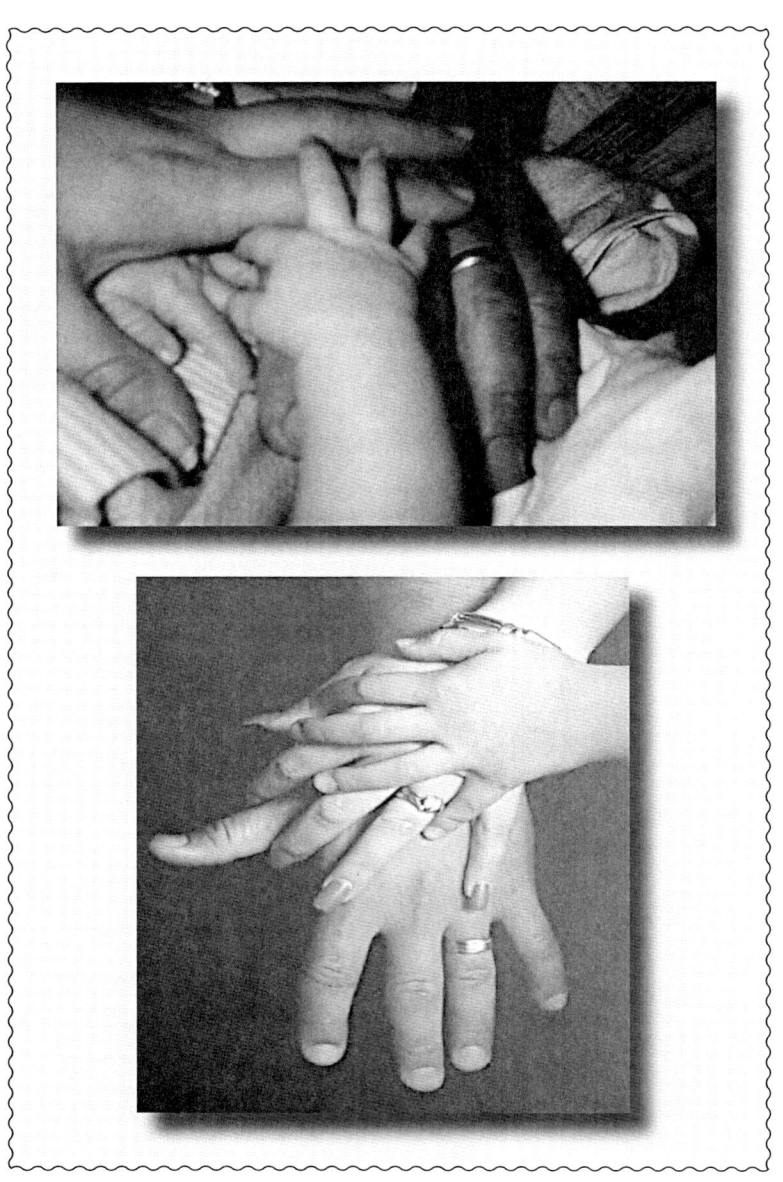

JRD - 5/20/1998 (top)
JRD - 11/6/2005 (bottom)

Epilogue

I'll sign off with this wonderful poem. I wish I could locate the author, but I have searched every place I know and cannot seem to locate their name to give them proper credit. So in their honor for writing such a beautiful gift to all parents, and in your honor for taking the time to become a better parent, I leave you with this...

The Last Time

*From the moment you hold your baby in your arms,
you will never be the same.
You might long for the person you were before,
When you had freedom and time,
And nothing in particular to worry about.*

*You will know tiredness like you never knew it before,
And days will run into days that are exactly the same,
Full of feedings and burping,
Nappy changes and crying,
Whining and fighting,
Naps or a lack of naps,
It might seem like a never-ending cycle.*

*But remember ...
There is a last time for everything.
There will come a time when you will feed
your baby for the very last time.
They will fall asleep on you after a long day
And it will be the last time you ever hold your sleeping child.*

*One day you will carry them on your hip then set them down,
And never pick them up that way again.
You will scrub their hair in the bath one night*

EPILOGUE

And from that day on they will want to bathe alone.
They will hold your hand to cross the road,
Then never reach for it again.
They will creep into your room at midnight for cuddles,
And it will be the last night you ever wake to this.

One afternoon you will sing "the wheels on the bus"
and do all the actions,
Then never sing them that song again.
They will kiss you goodbye at the school gate,
The next day they will ask to walk to the gate alone.
You will read a final bedtime story
and wipe your last dirty face.
They will run to you with arms raised for the very last time.

The thing is, you won't even know it's the last time
Until there are no more times.
And even then, it will take you a while to realize.

So while you are living in these times,
remember there are only so many of them
and when they are gone,
you will yearn for just one more day of them.
For one last time.

-Author Unknown-

Song: As Easy As Our Blessings
Written by Tony Martin and Mark Nessler
Performed by Tracy Lawrence

Acknowledgments

When "Thank You" Just Isn't Enough...

John:
Everything I wrote in Dalton's journal was true then,
and it still is now...
Even though you question yourself all the time,
Dalton really was blessed to have you for his Daddy.
I could not have asked for a better
man to share my life with, to father my only child,
to live through this heartbreak for the rest of our existence.
You are the wizard of all things me, my lover, my everything.
I am proud to be your wife every second of every day.
I couldn't ask for more,
except that Dalton be here to share it with us.
For life, and ever after, I love you.
To infinity! And beyond!

Daxton:
You arrived just in time for all the chaos
and you're the best puppy in all the world!
Thank you for loving Dalton so much
and continuing to remind us that he is still here.
We couldn't have made it here without your unconditional love.

Mama Jean:
Thank you for having that seventh baby so many years ago.
I am so blessed to have the very best one for my husband,
and Dalton is so lucky to have him for his Daddy!
We are continually amazed by your strength each and every day.
Thank you for showing us what it's like
to keep going, and going, and going,
even when it feels like the world keeps kicking you down.
You are always an inspiration!
We love you to Texas and back, to infinity... and beyond...

Mom & Daddy:
The best parents a girl could ever have...
Thank you for everything;
all your guidance while I was growing up
and, especially now, as we struggle through each day.

ACKNOWLEDGMENTS

*Thank you for teaching me
about the healing power of music so early in life,
and for all the hours of travel,
tears, hugs, cuddles, cleaning, preparing food,
organizing people and lists and cards and gifts,
deposits and other work stuff,
spending the night when we couldn't be here alone,
and trusting us when we thought it was time
we do it on our own.
We would never have made it this far without you
and your undying support and love.
We love you beyond words, to infinity... and beyond...*

*Shauna:
I am so proud of the woman you've become
and the amazing sister you have continued to be
throughout our lives together.
Thanks for being so upbeat and positive
and for reminding me of all the good things
when it gets so dark in my head.
Thank you for still looking up to me
even when your heels have you standing 6" over my head.
I love you to infinity, and beyond,
to the moon and back, sis.
Thank you for being mine
and for sharing Fabricio and the kids with us!*

Molly:
GMS.
Thank you for being the best darn grief counselor
I don't have to pay for,
and the best "Wifey" John and I could ever have.
Your amazing grace, wisdom,
and subtle ways of helping me organize
and re-organize my jumbled thoughts
are some of the biggest blessings I could ever imagine.
I've never met anyone with a more beautiful heart and soul.
I am so blessed that you came into my life
and continue to want to be in it.
Jack and Caroline are amazing people,
all due to your remarkable skills as a mother.
John and I are so lucky to have all three of you in our lives.
Thank you for everything!
ILYTIAB! GN XOXOXOXO.

The Brown Family:
See? I told you moving into BHE
would change your life forever.
Now, you're stuck with us, and we love you for it!

ACKNOWLEDGMENTS

Kelly:
There are no words to give enough thanks
for everything you have been for us...
Thank you for being there with John and Dalton
while the medical team worked so hard trying to save him,
for getting John back to the camper,
for explaining what happened to me
in words I could sort-of understand,
for making all the phone calls
and taking my phone to continue conversations
when I could no longer speak,
for getting your family (Thank you, Hiniker's!)
to help move us from Glamis to Rio Bend,
while we waited four more excruciating days
to see Dalton again,
for locating Dalton's bike after they towed it away,
and for getting us home, all while being our rock,
knowing you had just lost your shadow...
Thank you.

Sonya:
I will never forget standing in the doorway of our camper,
looking over at you standing in yours,
still not understanding what John was trying to tell me,
as Kelly told you the news and took Brennan from your arms,
seeing you fall to the floor.

It's forever etched in my brain.
Thank you for all the calls you made, keeping everyone fed,
holding us when we couldn't comprehend reality,
taking care of Brennan and Dax,
and keeping it all together
when you had just lost your best little buddy.
Your friendship and strength have meant so much.
Thank you.

Brennan, Our Little Brownie:
How fitting that the very last picture we have of Dalton
is with you sitting on his lap,
as if to tell us that you will help guide us out of this darkness.
You have been a blessing beyond measure for Uncle John and I.
Your constant love and "squeeze our stuffin's out" hugs
remind us that you are a reason to keep going.
You really are our new sunshine.
Thank you, Boo-Bear.
We love you more than you'll ever know...

Sam & Nico:
While we know Dalton wasn't perfect (he was close),
he was made better by having both of you in his life.
Thank you for being his closest friends.
Dalton would be so happy

ACKNOWLEDGMENTS

*that you two are such good buddies now.
It means the world to us that you still
come around and spend time with us.
Thanks for all the hugs, the stories, and the listening,
and for still letting me measure how tall you are on the door,
even though you're all grown up now.
We are very proud of the exceptional young men
that you have become.
Thank you for continuing to be in our lives.
We love you both.*

*Beverly Hillbillies:
You all know how much the movie
Pay It Forward means to our family
and the candlelight homecoming
was much like the end of the movie.
Thank you all for giving our Angel the tribute
he so deserved for the big, beautiful life he lived
in such a short amount of time.
Thank you all for your help unloading and cleaning the camper,
and fixing the frozen pipes
during the coldest days in Colorado history.
There is no greater neighborhood than BHE!*

The Fidino Family:
Your friendship and support through the years
has been amazing.
While you guys tend to fly a bit under the radar,
please know that we see you,
we love you, and we appreciate you
more than you can imagine.

The Ravsten Family:
Who else could we have ever asked to do the unthinkable;
telling my family the tragic news?
That took more courage than we could ever imagine.
Thank you for handling all the text and email communications
while we tried to figure out details of getting Dalton home,
for allowing me the time off to handle Dalton's service,
and then rush off to Texas for Bill's service,
and for being patient with me through it all.
Thank you.

The Lujan Family:
It is baffling to know the pain you all have suffered
in each of your lives,
yet you still find beauty in life

ACKNOWLEDGMENTS

*and sharing what you've learned with others.
John and I have learned so much
from each and every one of you
in how to face our new existence head-on.
Thank you for teaching us that it's not about us,
but rather what we do with the experience that matters.
You've all been an amazing gift to both of us.
Thank you would never be enough...*

*Jenni-Lu:
Watching you as a friend, mother,
and special needs teacher
has been a huge learning experience.
I took every ounce of it you shared
and applied it to my life as a mother.
Thank you for all your wisdom,
especially in the early years!
Michael, Quentin, and Shelby
are all wonderful mini-you's
and we're so happy
you're all such a big part of our lives!*

*Linn & Ed:
Thank you both for all your parenting of us girls
while we were in junior high and high school
and for the plethora of beautiful words
and loving support
since Dalton left for Heaven.*

Chris & Michelle:
*Thank you for teaching the world about perfect love
in more ways than either of you even realize.*

Jon:
*Thank you for your long friendship,
beautiful smile, and huge spirit;
for protecting our country as a proud U.S. Marine;
for serving as a competitor in the U.S. Paralympics
and Triumph Games;
and for showing the world that hard work
and determination really do make the man.
Thank you for honoring Dalton on the slopes in Soji.
What an honor that he and Tibby
both got to ski down the mountain with a true Olympian!*

Lyss:
*I am so sorry that you've had to walk
the long path of grief ahead of John and I.
Thank you for so gracefully sharing
your love and experiences with us.
Tibby and Malcolm are blessed to have you as their Mommy!*

ACKNOWLEDGMENTS

Aunt Luane:
Thanks for all your help with the worksheet
and the discussion guide
and for all your amazing support throughout my life.
I love you.

Char:
You are my sunshine, my only sunshine.
You make me happy when skies are blue and gray and yellow and orange
and all the other colors.
I love you!

Kasie:
So many years... So many memories...
Time moved so fast back then,
yet so incredibly slow now.
Thank you for always being the strong one.
Love you.

Keira:
Yes, Keir-bear, I promise... Love you.

Mrs. Phelan, Ms. Boland, and Mrs. Spurlin:
Thank you for all you do for the students of Douglas County.
We nominate all of you for Teacher-of-a-Lifetime
because you all made such a huge difference in Dalton's education;
each of you teaching him that there really are great teachers out there
who really care about their students.
He loved each and every one of you for different reasons,
but the equivalent factor
was that he really felt as if you all cared about him.
Thank you for making such a huge difference in his life
at times when he (and we) needed it most.

All the Parents of Angels
who have helped us along our grief journey:
While we wish you didn't have to,
thank you for paving our way.
Your knowledge of the grief process
and the pain has helped us to know
that we're not as lost as we feel like we are.
We continually do our best to help others
along this dark path too,
Paying It Forward for all of our Angels.
Thank you.

ACKNOWLEDGMENTS

Polly:
I know you were thinking a Pay It Forward book
would have been a better topic,
but that one was already written.
I hope you're okay with this one instead.
Thank you for taking your time to come see me speak
to the students at RHMS,
for all the brunches and brilliant advice,
for the amazing classes from My Word Publishing,
for all the great connections, for all the Gold Stars,
and for listening and believing
that this was an effective way to honor Dalton.
Hugs!

Polly's Team:
Donna, Pamela, Britt, Susie, Victoria, Vicki, Andrea, Adam, and Gail:
Thank you for listening to my story
and then reading all my crazy idea emails,
to create our masterpiece cover and interior design.
Your thoughtful comments were all
well received and much appreciated.
You are all Rock Stars!

Cindi & Scott @ Ecographics:
Thank you for printing all the programs,
letters, and PIF cards,
and for all your help with the journal.
Your efforts have touched many lives
stretching from here,
across the U.S., and over the borders.
Thank you
sooooooooooooooooooooo very much!

Aaron @ KSB Die Cutting & Luann @ Your Bindery:
Since the journal won't have a section for thank you's,
I wanted to squeeze them in here...
First and foremost, Lu,
thank you for hiring me all those years ago
and teaching me how to drive a stick shift,
and thank you for allowing Aaron to hang out
with an "older girl" in high school.
Secondly, thank you both for all your help
trying to figure out my journal idea.
Let's hope it makes a huge impact
on parents and kids all over the world!
Love you guys!

ACKNOWLEDGMENTS

Andy & Angie:
Thank you for handling the photos,
videos, and music at the celebration,
and for taking so many beautiful family photos
for us all those years ago.
We still remember taking the cover shot
laying in the leaves by Shauna's house.
Thank you for letting us use it for the cover.
Love you both.

To Everyone Who Has Reached Out:
Please know that we appreciate
every single card, letter, email,
phone call, voice mail, text, and Facebook post,
even when you don't know what to say
(because there's nothing that can be said
that makes this better).
Just knowing you're around if we need a shoulder to cry on,
or to help when our foggy brains aren't working,
makes all the difference.

*We could go on and on for days
thanking the many people
who have helped us on our journey, so we'll stop here.
Please know if you're name was not mentioned,
it's not that you were forgotten,
only that we ran out of room.*

*With much love and many hugs,
and more appreciation than could ever be said here,
Roni & John*

> Song: Because You Loved Me
> Songwriter: Diane Warren
> Performed by Celine Dion

Discussion Guide

(Also available on my website in pdf format.)

These discussion questions are meant to help you and your loved ones discuss and better understand your roles with the children in your lives, as well as to assist you in becoming more successful in your roles.

General
- ♥ How did this book impact you emotionally?
- ♥ On a scale of 1-10 (10 being very effective), how would you rate yourself as a parent?
  - ♥ What do you wish you had done better?
  - ♥ What do you wish you had done differently?
  - ♥ In what areas have you been a good parent?

- ♥ What have you done well?
- ♥ What will you change/implement after reading this book?
- ♥ What have you done well to show your children that you love them?
- ♥ What have you done well to guide your children toward happiness?

Schedules
- ♥ Have you asked your children if they are happy with their schedules (school, sports, lessons, tutoring, etc.)?
- ♥ Have you asked your children what they would like to change, if anything, about their daily schedules?
- ♥ Do they feel like they are too busy to be a kid, or do they wish they had extra-curricular activities to keep them busier?

Implementation - Discuss the use of the worksheet as a tool to help you begin the process.
- ♥ Not every idea mentioned in the book will work for every family. What ideas seem particularly relevant and attainable for you?
- ♥ What benefits do you hope to achieve by implementing some of the ideas?

- ♥ How do you think your children will react if you implement the ideas?
- ♥ What obstacles do you think you will face as you try to implement the ideas?
- ♥ How many new practices do you want to try to implement in the coming year?
- ♥ How will you make that happen?
- ♥ How will you hold yourself accountable?
  - ♥ Spouse/Partner
  - ♥ Buddy system
  - ♥ Being fully engaged
  - ♥ Other
- ♥ How will you know if you were successful in implementing the ideas you chose?

Daily Life
- ♥ Quickly jot down your typical schedule for weekdays and weekends.
  - ♥ Do you see any spots of "free time" that you could use on a weekly basis to have 30 minutes to yourself to read, write, craft, play an instrument, exercise, etc.?
  - ♥ Do you see any spots of "free time" that you could use to spend 5-10 minutes with each child offering them your absolute undivided attention (no phones or electronics)?

- ♥ If there's no "free time" available, could you re-arrange your schedule to fit that time in, even if you started incrementally?
- ♥ What are some of the "tools" you use to make life easier for yourself and your family?
- ♥ What are some other "tools" you wish were available to help with the daily stresses of your life?
- ♥ Who cooks and cleans at your house?
  - ♥ Could you share any of those chores with the kids or your spouse/partner/roommates?
  - ♥ Are there ways these chores could be made fun (make finding cooking ingredients into a game, create your own recipes together based on ingredients you already have, etc.)?
  - ♥ If you *did* share the chores, would the "*have to* make dinner" become "*get to* make dinner" because you're doing it together?
  - ♥ Would sharing chores give you the opportunity to have more time together after the chores were done?
- ♥ Do your children have cell phones or other electronics they use regularly?
  - ♥ Is your child responsible in their use of these devices?
  - ♥ What responsibilities do they have? (Do they pay their own phone bill? Do they know when

to turn it off and enjoy the here and now?)
- ♥ What are the rules in your house regarding these devices?
- ♥ What are the struggles you face most often regarding these devices?
- ♥ Are the struggles worth the benefits/convenience these devices offer?

Mornings
- ♥ How does a typical morning usually play out at your house?
- ♥ Are your mornings calm or hectic?
- ♥ Do you make time to cuddle/tickle/talk with each of your children before getting them up for the day?
- ♥ If you drive the kids to daycare or school, do you use that time to talk/sing with them?
- ♥ What would help make mornings more enjoyable?
- ♥ How could you implement better strategies to make mornings go more smoothly?

Eating Out
- ♥ When you go out to a restaurant to eat, how do you and your kids behave?
  - ♥ Are phones/electronics turned off or left at home/in the car?

- ♥ Are you more lenient/more strict with phones/electronics at a restaurant than you are at home?
  - ♥ Is everyone required to eat everything on their plate, or is it okay to stop when they get full?
- ♥ Have you ever stopped to look at other families to see if they are communicating at dinner?
  - ♥ If you see another family not communicating, how does that make you feel?
  - ♥ Does seeing other families not communicating with each other help you see the importance of putting down your devices and paying attention to those there with you?
- ♥ Are there things you could implement that would make eating out more fun for your family?

Bedtime Rituals
- ♥ Do you have a specific bedtime for your kids?
- ♥ How long does it take from the start of your bedtime rituals until you actually get to crawl into bed yourself?
- ♥ Are there specific steps you take each night to get the kids and yourself to bed (teeth-brushing, baths, stories, songs, highs-lows, journals, etc.)?
- ♥ What's the last thing your kids say to you before they go to sleep?

DISCUSSION GUIDE

♥ What's the last thing you say to your kids before they go to sleep?

Feel free to send your ideas for other questions and topics to DoItForDalton@gmail.com.

Please visit
www.ParentingAtYourBestWithoutRegrets.com
for the most updated discussion topics.

The Soundtrack of Our Lives With Dalton

Song	Artist	Songwriters
When I See You Smile	Bad English	Diane Warren
Rich Man	Mark Wills	Rory Lee and David Vincent Williams
You'll Be In My Heart	Phil Collins	Phil Collins
You're Gonna Miss This	Trace Adkins	Ashley Gorley & Lee Thomas Miller
(They Long to Be) Close to You	The Carpenters	Burt Bacharach and Hal David
The Dollar	Jamey Johnson	Jamey Johnson
Count On Me	Bruno Mars	Bruno Mars, Philip Lawrence, and Ari Levine
Little Hercules	Trisha Yearwood	Craig D. Carothers
Watching You	Rodney Atkins	Rodney Atkins, Steve Dean, and Brian Gene White
Heart To Heart (Stelen's Song)	Toby Keith	Toby Keith
I Hope You Dance	Lee Ann Womack	Mark Sanders and Tia Sillers
Sowin' Love	Paul Overstreet	Paul Overstreet and Don Schlitz
Humble and Kind	Tim McGraw	Lori McKenna
My Wish	Rascal Flatts	Jeffrey Steele and Steve Robson
Coat of Many Colors	Dolly Parton	Dolly Parton
Where Does The Money Come From	Tonic Sol-Fa	Kevin Fisher and Fred Wilhelm
Nothin' Grows In Shadows	Jake Owen	Rhett Akins, Dallas Davidson, Doug Johnson
It Won't Be Like this For Long	Darius Rucker	Darius Rucker, Chris DuBois, Ashley Gorley
Celebration	Kool & the Gang	Kool & the Gang

Song	Artist	Songwriters
Cheeseburger In Paradise	Jimmy Buffett	Jimmy Buffett
In Color	Jamey Johnson	Jamey Johnson, Lee Thomas Miller, James Otto
I Learned It From The Radio	Thomas Rhett	Nicolle Galyon, Ashley Gorley, and Jimmy Robbins
Like There's No Yesterday	Mark Wills	Chris Lindsey, Aimee Mayo, Troy Verges, Brett James
Smile	Uncle Kracker	Uncle Kracker, Blair Daly, J.T. Harding, and Jeremy Bose
Anything Like Me	Brad Paisley	Brad Paisley, Charles Dubois, and Dave Turnbull
Convoy	C.W. McCall	C.W. McCall and Chip Davis
If Everyone Cared	Nickelback	Chad Kroeger, Michael Kroeger, Ryan Peake, Ryan Anthony, Daniel Adair
Don't Blink	Kenny Chesney	Chris Allen Wallin and Casey Michael Beathard
The Chain of Love	Clay Walker	Clay Walker & Rory Feek
Lean On Me	Bill Withers	Bill Withers
Voices	Chris Young	Chris Young, Chris Tompkins, Craig Wiseman
You'll Always Be My Baby	Sara Evans	Sara Evans, Tom Shapiro, Tony Martin
Send 'Em On Down the Road	Garth Brooks	Marc Beeson and Allen Shamblin
As Easy As Our Blessings	Tracy Lawrence	Tony Martin and Mark Nessler
Because You Loved Me	Celine Dion	Diane Warren

Christmas - 12/25/2012 (top)
Walden Sand Dunes - July 2013 (bottom)

Author Bio

Known as a serial entrepreneur by her family and friends, Roni Wing Lambrecht has always been a forward thinker, spending her time working on projects to make life easier and more organized for everyone she connects with. Roni has run her own mortgage document preparation and closing company since 1996 and has been a REALTOR® since 2008.

Roni and her husband, John, have been married since 1995. Their beautiful son, Dalton, was with them for 15 years and left for Heaven just after Christmas 2013 due to injuries from an ATV accident. Dalton lived his short life creating smiles, laughter, and happiness by sharing his kind spirit and helping others through tough times. Roni and John continue his legacy by counting their blessings for the short time they had him and practicing random acts of kindness in his memory each and every day.

Roni and John live in Castle Rock, Colorado with their dog, Daxton. They spend most of their time remodeling and selling homes for their clients. Any free time is spent with their families in Colorado and Texas, and riding ATVs and camping in sand dunes across the U.S.

Roni's books, *Parenting At Your Best, A Parent's Journal to Their Child,* and *A Parent's Guide for Journaling to Their Child* are a tribute to Dalton, with anticipation that the stories and advice they offer will inspire others to excellence in their parenting.

If this book has helped you in any way,
please share it with someone else.
It makes a great gift for weddings,
baby showers, birthdays, and just because!

Thank you for sharing.

Additional parenting resources can be found at
www.ParentingAtYourBestWithoutRegrets.com

We welcome your comments.
Please email DoItForDalton@gmail.com
and put "Book" in the subject line.

We also welcome your reviews and endorsements.
Please post them on Amazon.com.

For speaking engagements or book club visits,
please email DoItForDalton@gmail.com.